CW01091549

You Don't Know JS Yet: Scope & Closures

Kyle Simpson

You Don't Know JS Yet: Scope & Closures

Kyle Simpson

ISBN 979-8-62153-645-9

Published by GetiPub (http://getipub.com), a division of Getify Solutions, Inc., and produced by Leanpub (https://leanpub.com/fljs).

Editor: Simon St.Laurent Copy Editor: Jasmine Kwityn Cover Art: David Neal (@reverentgeek)

March 2020: Second Edition

Revision History for the Second Edition

2020-03-03: First Release

While the publisher and the author have used good faith efforts to ensure that the information and instructions contained in this work are accurate, the publisher and the author disclaim all responsibility for errors or omissions, including without limitation responsibility for damages resulting from the use of or reliance on this work. Use of the information and instructions contained in this work is at your own risk. If any code samples or other technology this work contains or describes is subject to open source licenses or the intellectual property rights of others, it is your responsibility to ensure that your use thereof complies with such licenses and/or rights.

© 2020 Getify Solutions, Inc.

I must first thank my wife and kids, whose constant support is what allows me to keep going. I also want to thank the 500 original backers of the Kickstarter for "You Don't Know JS" (1st ed), as well as the hundreds of thousands of folks who bought and read those books since. Without your financial support, this second edition wouldn't be happening. Thanks also to the interviewer at a certain avian social media company who said I didn't "know enough about JS"... you helped me name the series.

Next, I owe much of my current career path to Marc Grabanski and Frontend Masters. Marc took a chance on me and gave me my first shot at teaching years ago, and I wouldn't have then become a writer had it not been for that! Frontend Masters is the Premier Sponsor of YDKJSY 2nd Edition. Thank you, Frontend Masters (and Marc).

Lastly, my editor, Simon St.Laurent, who helped me conceive the original YDKJS and was my first book editor. Simon's support and guidance have profoundly impacted me and been an integral part of shaping me into the writer I am today. From those drinks we enjoyed at the Driskill all those years back, where YDKJS was born, through today, thank you so much Simon for shepherding and improving these books!

Contents

FrontendMasters

Frontend Masters is the premier sponsor of the 2nd edition of the *You Don't Know JS Yet* book series.

Frontend Masters helps you advance your skills with in-depth, modern front-end engineering courses, the highest quality video content available anywhere on the web. With over 150 courses to choose from, the expert content you need to take your development to the next level is here, so get started by joining today!

https://frontendmasters.com/join

Among the amazing courses in the Frontend Masters library, Kyle's courses are the perfect companion materials to this book series. Check them all out, including these few specifically:

- Getting Started with JavaScript
- Deep JavaScript Foundations
- JavaScript: The Recent Parts

https://frontendmasters.com/kyle-simpson

Foreword

If I look over the books on my bookshelf, I can clearly see which of these titles are well loved. Well loved in this sense meaning they are a little worn. Their binding is broken, their pages are tattered, there might even be a spilled drink smear or two. What's ironic to me is that the most loved of my books often ***look*** the least cared for, though honestly the opposite is true.

Scope and Closures (1st ed.) is one of my most loved books. It's small, but the binding is coming undone. The pages are worn and dog-eared. It's a bit rumpled. It's not a book I've read once. I've picked it up again and again in the many years since it was originally published.

For me, it's also been a benchmark for my own personal progression through JavaScript. When I first read it in 2014, I was familiar with the concepts but the depth of my understanding was admittedly not as deep as the thin volume.

Over the years, even though I wasn't necessarily feeling my own improvement on a day-to-day basis, each one of the concepts became more approachable. I'd smile to myself, realizing how far I'd come with the help of these guides. It became apparent there was an inverse correlation between how well I treated the book and how much I loved it.

When Kyle asked me to write the Foreword for the 2nd edition, I was floored. It's not often you're asked to write about a book that's been so formative for your own understanding and career, *Scope and Closures* in particular. I remember the day I first understood closures, the first time I used one well. The satisfaction was great, in part because the symmetry of the idea was compelling to me. Before I even picked this book up, I was already enamoured with closures. And yet, there's a difference between being able to execute code successfully and fully explore the concepts with any depth. This book took my base understanding and drew it out, helped me master it.

This book is deceptively short. It's helpful that it's small because it's dense with useful knowledge. Since it is compact, I'd suggest you give yourself time to absorb each page. Take your time with it. Treat the book with care, and by that I mean, wear it down.

~~

Sarah Drasner

Head of Developer Experience

Netlify

Preface

Welcome to the 2nd edition of the widely acclaimed *You Don't Know JS* (**YDKJS**) book series: *You Don't Know JS* ***Yet*** (**YDKJSY**).

If you've read any of the 1st edition books, you can expect a refreshed approach in these new ones, with plenty of updated coverage of what's changed in JS over the last five years. But what I hope and believe you'll still *get* is the same commitment to respecting JS and digging into what really makes it tick.

If this is your first time reading these books, I'm glad you're here. Prepare for a deep and extensive journey into all the corners of JavaScript.

If you are new to programming or JS, be aware that these books are not intended as a gentle "intro to JavaScript." This material is, at times, complex and challenging, and goes much deeper than is typical for a first-time learner. You're welcome here no matter what your background is, but these books are written assuming you're already comfortable with JS and have at least 6–9 months experience with it.

The Parts

These books approach JavaScript intentionally opposite of how *The Good Parts* treats the language. No, that doesn't mean we're looking at *the bad parts*, but rather, exploring **all the parts**.

You may have been told, or felt yourself, that JS is a deeply flawed language that was poorly designed and inconsistently implemented. Many have asserted that it's the worst most popular language in the world; that nobody writes JS because they want to, only because they have to given its place at the center of the web. That's a ridiculous, unhealthy, and wholly condescending claim.

Millions of developers write JavaScript every day, and many of them appreciate and respect the language.

Like any great language, it has its brilliant parts as well as its scars. Even the creator of JavaScript himself, Brendan Eich, laments some of those parts as mistakes. But he's wrong: they weren't mistakes at all. JS is what it is today—the world's most ubiquitous and thus most influential programming language—precisely because of *all those parts*.

Don't buy the lie that you should only learn and use a small collection of *good parts* while avoiding all the bad stuff. Don't buy the "X is the new Y" snake oil, that some new feature of the language instantly relegates all usage of a previous feature as obsolete and ignorant. Don't listen when someone says your code isn't "modern" because it isn't yet using a stage-0 feature that was only proposed a few weeks ago!

Every part of JS is useful. Some parts are more useful than others. Some parts require you to be more careful and intentional.

I find it absurd to try to be a truly effective JavaScript developer while only using a small sliver of what the language has to offer. Can you imagine a construction worker with a toolbox full of tools, who only uses their hammer and scoffs at the screwdriver or tape measure as inferior? That's just silly.

My unreserved claim is that you should go about learning all parts of JavaScript, and where appropriate, use them! And if I may be so bold as to suggest: it's time to discard any JS books that tell you otherwise.

The Title?

So what's the title of the series all about?

I'm not trying to insult you with criticism about your current lack of knowledge or understanding of JavaScript. I'm not suggesting you can't or won't be able to learn JavaScript. I'm not boasting about secret advanced insider wisdom that I and only a select few possess.

Seriously, all those were real reactions to the original series title before folks even read the books. And they're baseless.

The primary point of the title "You Don't Know JS Yet" is to point out that most JS developers don't take the time to really understand how the code that they write works. They know *that* it works—that it produces a desired outcome. But they either don't understand exactly *how*, or worse, they have an inaccurate mental model for the *how* that falters on closer scrutiny.

I'm presenting a gentle but earnest challenge to you the reader, to set aside the assumptions you have about JS, and approach it with fresh eyes and an invigorated curiosity that leads you to ask *why* for every line of code you write. Why does it do what it does? Why is one way better or more appropriate than the other half-dozen ways you could have accomplished it?

Why do all the "popular kids" say to do X with your code, but it turns out that Y might be a better choice?

I added "Yet" to the title, not only because it's the second edition, but because ultimately I want these books to challenge you in a hopeful rather than discouraging way.

But let me be clear: I don't think it's possible to ever fully *know* JS. That's not an achievement to be obtained, but a goal to strive after. You don't finish knowing everything about JS, you just keep learning more and more as you spend more time with the language. And the deeper you go, the more you revisit what you *knew* before, and you re-learn it from that more experienced perspective.

I encourage you to adopt a mindset around JavaScript, and indeed all of software development, that you will never fully have mastered it, but that you can and should keep working to get closer to that end, a journey that will stretch for the entirety of your software development career, and beyond.

You can always know JS better than you currently do. That's what I hope these YDKJSY books represent.

The Mission

The case doesn't really need to be made for why developers should take JS seriously—I think it's already more than proven worthy of first-class status among the world's programming languages.

But a different, more important case still needs to be made, and these books rise to that challenge.

I've taught more than 5,000 developers from teams and companies all over the world, in more than 25 countries on six continents. And what I've seen is that far too often, what *counts* is generally just the result of the program, not how the program is written or how/why it works.

My experience not only as a developer but in teaching many other developers tells me: you will always be more effective in your development work if you more completely understand how your code works than you are solely *just* getting it to produce a desired outcome.

In other words, *good enough to work* is not, and should not be, *good enough.*

All developers regularly struggle with some piece of code not working correctly, and they can't figure out why. But far too often, JS developers will blame this on the language rather than admitting it's their own understanding that is falling short. These books serve as both the question and answer: why did it do *this*, and here's how to get it to do *that* instead.

My mission with YDKJSY is to empower every single JS developer to fully own the code they write, to understand it and to write with intention and clarity.

The Path

Some of you have started reading this book with the goal of completing all six books, back to back.

I would like to caution you to consider changing that plan.

It is not my intention that YDKJSY be read straight through. The material in these books is dense, because JavaScript is powerful, sophisticated, and in parts rather complex. Nobody can really hope to *download* all this information to their brains in a single pass and retain any significant amount of it. That's unreasonable, and it's foolish to try.

My suggestion is you take your time going through YDKJSY. Take one chapter, read it completely through start to finish, and then go back and re-read it section by section. Stop in between each section, and practice the code or ideas from that section. For larger concepts, it probably is a good idea to expect to spend several days digesting, re-reading, practicing, then digesting some more.

You could spend a week or two on each chapter, and a month or two on each book, and a year or more on the whole series, and you would still not be squeezing every ounce of YDKJSY out.

Don't binge these books; be patient and spread out your reading. Interleave reading with lots of practice on real code in your job or on projects you participate in. Wrestle with the opinions I've presented along the way, debate with others, and most of all, disagree with me! Run a study group or book club. Teach mini-workshops at your office. Write blog posts on what you've learned. Speak about these topics at local JS meetups.

It's never my goal to convince you to agree with my opinion, but to encourage you to own and be able to defend your opinions. You can't get *there* with an expedient read-through of these books. That's something that takes a long while to emerge, little by little, as you study and ponder and re-visit.

These books are meant to be a field-guide on your wanderings through JavaScript, from wherever you currently are with the language, to a place of deeper understanding. And the deeper you understand JS, the more questions you will ask and the more you will have to explore! That's what I find so exciting!

I'm so glad you're embarking on this journey, and I am so honored you would consider and consult these books along the way. It's time to start *getting to know JS*.

Chapter 1: What's the Scope?

By the time you've written your first few programs, you're likely getting somewhat comfortable with creating variables and storing values in them. Working with variables is one of the most foundational things we do in programming!

But you may not have considered very closely the underlying mechanisms used by the engine to organize and manage these variables. I don't mean how the memory is allocated on the computer, but rather: how does JS know which variables are accessible by any given statement, and how does it handle two variables of the same name?

The answers to questions like these take the form of well-defined rules called scope. This book will dig through all aspects of scope—how it works, what it's useful for, gotchas to avoid—and then point toward common scope patterns that guide the structure of programs.

Our first step is to uncover how the JS engine processes our program **before** it runs.

About This Book

Welcome to book 2 in the *You Don't Know JS Yet* series! If you already finished *Get Started* (the first book), you're in the right spot! If not, before you proceed I encourage you to *start there* for the best foundation.

Our focus will be the first of three pillars in the JS language: the scope system and its function closures, as well as the power of the module design pattern.

JS is typically classified as an interpreted scripting language, so it's assumed by most that JS programs are processed in a single, top-down pass. But JS is in fact parsed/compiled in a separate phase **before execution begins**. The code author's decisions on where to place variables, functions, and blocks with respect to each other are analyzed according to the rules of scope, during the initial parsing/compilation phase. The resulting scope structure is generally unaffected by runtime conditions.

JS functions are themselves first-class values; they can be assigned and passed around just like numbers or strings. But since these functions hold and access variables, they maintain their original scope no matter where in the program the functions are eventually executed. This is called closure.

Modules are a code organization pattern characterized by public methods that have privileged access (via closure) to hidden variables and functions in the internal scope of the module.

Compiled vs. Interpreted

You may have heard of *code compilation* before, but perhaps it seems like a mysterious black box where source code slides in one end and executable programs pop out the other.

It's not mysterious or magical, though. Code compilation is a set of steps that process the text of your code and turn it into a list of instructions the computer can understand. Typically, the whole source code is transformed at once, and those resulting instructions are saved as output (usually in a file) that can later be executed.

You also may have heard that code can be *interpreted*, so how is that different from being *compiled*?

Interpretation performs a similar task to compilation, in that it transforms your program into machine-understandable instructions. But the processing model is different. Unlike a program being compiled all at once, with interpretation the source code is transformed line by line; each line or statement is executed before immediately proceeding to processing the next line of the source code.

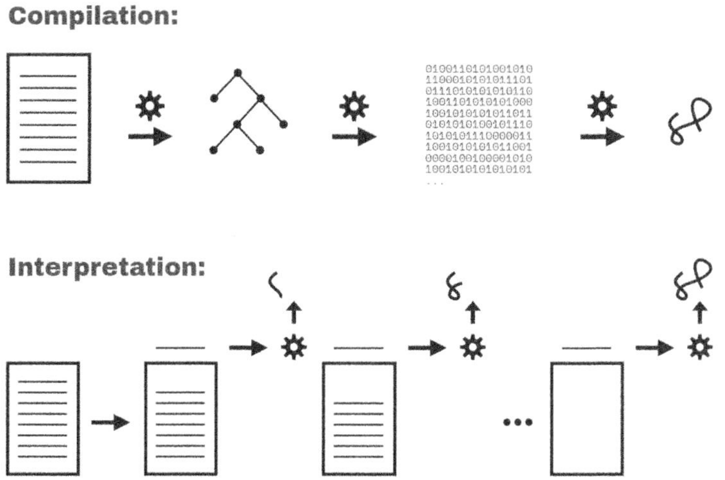

Fig. 1: Compiled vs. Interpreted Code

Figure 1 illustrates compilation vs. interpretation of programs.

Are these two processing models mutually exclusive? Generally, yes. However, the issue is more nuanced, because interpretation can actually take other forms than just operating line by line on source code text. Modern JS engines actually employ numerous variations of both compilation and interpretation in the handling of JS programs.

Recall that we surveyed this topic in Chapter 1 of the *Get Started* book. Our conclusion there is that JS is most accurately portrayed as a **compiled language**. For the benefit of readers here, the following sections will revisit and expand on that assertion.

Compiling Code

But first, why does it even matter whether JS is compiled or not?

Scope is primarily determined during compilation, so understanding how compilation and execution relate is key in mastering scope.

In classic compiler theory, a program is processed by a compiler in three basic stages:

1. **Tokenizing/Lexing**: breaking up a string of characters into meaningful (to the language) chunks, called tokens. For instance, consider the program: `var a = 2;`. This program would likely be broken up into the following tokens: `var`, `a`, `=`, `2`, and `;`. Whitespace may or may not be persisted as a token, depending on whether it's meaningful or not.

   (The difference between tokenizing and lexing is subtle and academic, but it centers on whether or not these tokens are identified in a *stateless* or *stateful* way. Put simply, if the tokenizer were to invoke stateful parsing rules to figure out whether `a` should be considered a distinct token or just part of another token, *that* would be **lexing**.)

2. **Parsing**: taking a stream (array) of tokens and turning it into a tree of nested elements, which collectively represent the grammatical structure of the program. This is called an Abstract Syntax Tree (AST).

   For example, the tree for `var a = 2;` might start with a top-level node called `VariableDeclaration`, with a child node called `Identifier` (whose value is `a`), and another child called `AssignmentExpression` which itself has a child called `NumericLiteral` (whose value is `2`).

3. **Code Generation**: taking an AST and turning it into executable code. This part varies greatly depending on the language, the platform it's targeting, and other factors.

   The JS engine takes the just described AST for `var a = 2;` and turns it into a set of machine instructions to actually *create* a variable called `a` (including reserving memory, etc.), and then store a value into `a`.

> **Note**
>
> The implementation details of a JS engine (utilizing system memory resources, etc.) is much deeper than we will dig here. We'll keep our focus on the observable behavior of our programs and let the JS engine manage those deeper system-level abstractions.

The JS engine is vastly more complex than *just* these three stages. In the process of parsing and code generation, there are steps to optimize the performance of the execution (i.e., collapsing redundant elements). In fact, code can even be recompiled and re-optimized during the progression of execution.

So, I'm painting only with broad strokes here. But you'll see shortly why *these* details we *do* cover, even at a high level, are relevant.

JS engines don't have the luxury of an abundance of time to perform their work and optimizations, because JS compilation doesn't happen in a build step ahead of time, as with other languages. It usually must happen in mere microseconds (or less!) right before the code is executed. To ensure the fastest performance under these constraints, JS engines use all kinds of tricks (like JITs, which lazy compile and even hot recompile); these are well beyond the "scope" of our discussion here.

Required: Two Phases

To state it as simply as possible, the most important observation we can make about processing of JS programs is that it occurs in (at least) two phases: parsing/compilation first, then execution.

The separation of a parsing/compilation phase from the subsequent execution phase is observable fact, not theory or opinion. While the JS specification does not require "compilation" explicitly, it requires behavior that is essentially only practical with a compile-then-execute approach.

There are three program characteristics you can observe to prove this to yourself: syntax errors, early errors, and hoisting.

Syntax Errors from the Start

Consider this program:

```
var greeting = "Hello";

console.log(greeting);

greeting = ."Hi";
// SyntaxError: unexpected token .
```

This program produces no output (`"Hello"` is not printed), but instead throws a `SyntaxError` about the unexpected `.` token right before the `"Hi"` string. Since the syntax error happens after the well-formed `console.log(..)` statement, if JS was executing top-down line by line, one would expect the `"Hello"` message being printed before the syntax error being thrown. That doesn't happen.

In fact, the only way the JS engine could know about the syntax error on the third line, before executing the first and second lines, is by the JS engine first parsing the entire program before any of it is executed.

Early Errors

Next, consider:

```
console.log("Howdy");

saySomething("Hello","Hi");
// Uncaught SyntaxError: Duplicate parameter name not
// allowed in this context

function saySomething(greeting,greeting) {
    "use strict";
    console.log(greeting);
}
```

The `"Howdy"` message is not printed, despite being a well-formed statement.

Instead, just like the snippet in the previous section, the `SyntaxError` here is thrown before the program is executed. In this case, it's because strict-mode (opted in for only the `saySomething(..)` function here) forbids, among many other things, functions to have duplicate parameter names; this has always been allowed in non-strict-mode.

The error thrown is not a syntax error in the sense of being a malformed string of tokens (like `."Hi"` prior), but in strict-mode is nonetheless required by the specification to be thrown as an "early error" before any execution begins.

But how does the JS engine know that the `greeting` parameter has been duplicated? How does it know that the `saySomething(..)` function is even in strict-mode while processing the parameter list (the `"use strict"` pragma appears only later, in the function body)?

Again, the only reasonable explanation is that the code must first be *fully* parsed before any execution occurs.

Hoisting

Finally, consider:

```
function saySomething() {
    var greeting = "Hello";
    {
        greeting = "Howdy";  // error comes from here
        let greeting = "Hi";
        console.log(greeting);
    }
}

saySomething();
// ReferenceError: Cannot access 'greeting' before
// initialization
```

The noted `ReferenceError` occurs from the line with the statement `greeting = "Howdy"`. What's happening is that the `greeting` variable for that statement belongs to the declaration on the next line, `let greeting = "Hi"`, rather than to the previous `var greeting = "Hello"` statement.

The only way the JS engine could know, at the line where the error is thrown, that the *next statement* would declare a block-scoped variable of the same name (`greeting`) is if the JS engine had already processed this code in an earlier pass, and already set up all the scopes and their variable associations. This processing of scopes and declarations can only accurately be accomplished by parsing the program before execution.

The `ReferenceError` here technically comes from `greeting = "Howdy"` accessing the `greeting` variable **too early**, a conflict referred to as the Temporal Dead Zone (TDZ). Chapter 5 will cover this in more detail.

> **Warning**
>
> It's often asserted that `let` and `const` declarations are not hoisted, as an explanation of the TDZ behavior just illustrated. But this is not accurate. We'll come back and explain both the hoisting and TDZ of `let`/`const` in Chapter 5.

Hopefully you're now convinced that JS programs are parsed before any execution begins. But does it prove they are compiled?

This is an interesting question to ponder. Could JS parse a program, but then execute that program by *interpreting* operations represented in the AST **without** first compiling the program? Yes, that is *possible*. But it's extremely unlikely, mostly because it would be extremely inefficient performance wise.

It's hard to imagine a production-quality JS engine going to all the trouble of parsing a program into an AST, but not then converting (aka, "compiling") that AST into the most efficient (binary) representation for the engine to then execute.

Many have endeavored to split hairs with this terminology, as there's plenty of nuance and "well, actually..." interjections floating around. But in spirit and in practice, what the engine is doing in processing JS programs is **much more alike compilation** than not.

Classifying JS as a compiled language is not concerned with the distribution model for its binary (or byte-code) executable representations, but rather in keeping a clear distinction in our minds about the phase where JS code is processed and analyzed; this phase observably and indisputedly happens *before* the code starts to be executed.

We need proper mental models of how the JS engine treats our code if we want to understand JS and scope effectively.

Compiler Speak

With awareness of the two-phase processing of a JS program (compile, then execute), let's turn our attention to how the JS engine identifies variables and determines the scopes of a program as it is compiled.

First, let's examine a simple JS program to use for analysis over the next several chapters:

```
var students = [
    { id: 14, name: "Kyle" },
    { id: 73, name: "Suzy" },
    { id: 112, name: "Frank" },
    { id: 6, name: "Sarah" }
];

function getStudentName(studentID) {
    for (let student of students) {
        if (student.id == studentID) {
            return student.name;
        }
    }
}
```

```
var nextStudent = getStudentName(73);

console.log(nextStudent);
// Suzy
```

Other than declarations, all occurrences of variables/identifiers in a program serve in one of two "roles": either they're the *target* of an assignment or they're the *source* of a value.

(When I first learned compiler theory while earning my computer science degree, we were taught the terms "LHS" (aka, *target*) and "RHS" (aka, *source*) for these roles, respectively. As you might guess from the "L" and the "R", the acronyms mean "Left-Hand Side" and "Right-Hand Side", as in left and right sides of an = assignment operator. However, assignment targets and sources don't always literally appear on the left or right of an =, so it's probably clearer to think in terms of *target / source* rather than *left / right*.)

How do you know if a variable is a *target*? Check if there is a value that is being assigned to it; if so, it's a *target*. If not, then the variable is a *source*.

For the JS engine to properly handle a program's variables, it must first label each occurrence of a variable as *target* or *source*. We'll dig in now to how each role is determined.

Targets

What makes a variable a *target*? Consider:

```
students = [ // ..
```

This statement is clearly an assignment operation; remember, the `var students` part is handled entirely as a declaration at compile time, and is thus irrelevant during execution; we left it out for clarity and focus. Same with the `nextStudent = getStudentName(73)` statement.

But there are three other *target* assignment operations in the code that are perhaps less obvious. One of them:

```
for (let student of students) {
```

That statement assigns a value to `student` for each iteration of the loop. Another *target* reference:

```
getStudentName(73)
```

But how is that an assignment to a *target*? Look closely: the argument `73` is assigned to the parameter `studentID`.

And there's one last (subtle) *target* reference in our program. Can you spot it?

..

..

..

Did you identify this one?

```
function getStudentName(studentID) {
```

A `function` declaration is a special case of a *target* reference. You can think of it sort of like `var getStudentName = function(studentID)`, but that's not exactly accurate. An identifier `getStudentName` is declared (at compile time), but the = `function(studentID)` part is also handled at compilation; the association between `getStudentName` and the function is automatically set up at the beginning of the scope rather than waiting for an = assignment statement to be executed.

> **Note**
>
> This automatic association of function and variable is referred to as "function hoisting", and is covered in detail in Chapter 5.

Sources

So we've identified all five *target* references in the program. The other variable references must then be *source* references (because that's the only other option!).

In `for (let student of students)`, we said that `student` is a *target*, but `students` is a *source* reference. In the statement `if (student.id == studentID)`, both `student` and `studentID` are *source* references. `student` is also a *source* reference in `return student.name`.

In `getStudentName(73)`, `getStudentName` is a *source* reference (which we hope resolves to a function reference value). In `console.log(nextStudent)`, `console` is a *source* reference, as is `nextStudent`.

> **Note**
>
> In case you were wondering, `id`, `name`, and `log` are all properties, not variable references.

What's the practical importance of understanding *targets* vs. *sources*? In Chapter 2, we'll revisit this topic and cover how a variable's role impacts its lookup (specifically, if the lookup fails).

Cheating: Runtime Scope Modifications

It should be clear by now that scope is determined as the program is compiled, and should not generally be affected by runtime conditions. However, in non-strict-mode, there are technically still two ways to cheat this rule, modifying a program's scopes during runtime.

Neither of these techniques *should* be used—they're both dangerous and confusing, and you should be using strict-mode (where they're disallowed) anyway. But it's important to be aware of them in case you run across them in some programs.

The `eval(..)` function receives a string of code to compile and execute on the fly during the program runtime. If that string of code has a `var` or `function` declaration in it, those declarations will modify the current scope that the `eval(..)` is currently executing in:

```
function badIdea() {
    eval("var oops = 'Ugh!';");
    console.log(oops);
}
badIdea();   // Ugh!
```

If the `eval(..)` had not been present, the `oops` variable in `console.log(oops)` would not exist, and would throw a

`ReferenceError`. But `eval(..)` modifies the scope of the `badIdea()` function at runtime. This is bad for many reasons, including the performance hit of modifying the already compiled and optimized scope, every time `badIdea()` runs.

The second cheat is the `with` keyword, which essentially dynamically turns an object into a local scope—its properties are treated as identifiers in that new scope's block:

```
var badIdea = { oops: "Ugh!" };

with (badIdea) {
    console.log(oops);    // Ugh!
}
```

The global scope was not modified here, but `badIdea` was turned into a scope at runtime rather than compile time, and its property `oops` becomes a variable in that scope. Again, this is a terrible idea, for performance and readability reasons.

At all costs, avoid `eval(..)` (at least, `eval(..)` creating declarations) and `with`. Again, neither of these cheats is available in strict-mode, so if you just use strict-mode (you should!) then the temptation goes away!

Lexical Scope

We've demonstrated that JS's scope is determined at compile time; the term for this kind of scope is "lexical scope". "Lexical" is associated with the "lexing" stage of compilation, as discussed earlier in this chapter.

To narrow this chapter down to a useful conclusion, the key idea of "lexical scope" is that it's controlled entirely by the placement of functions, blocks, and variable declarations, in relation to one another.

If you place a variable declaration inside a function, the compiler handles this declaration as it's parsing the function, and associates that declaration with the function's scope. If a variable is block-scope declared (`let` / `const`), then it's associated with the nearest enclosing `{ .. }` block, rather than its enclosing function (as with `var`).

Furthermore, a reference (*target* or *source* role) for a variable must be resolved as coming from one of the scopes that are *lexically available* to it; otherwise the variable is said to be "undeclared" (which usually results in an error!). If the variable is not declared in the current scope, the next outer/enclosing scope will be consulted. This process of stepping out one level of scope nesting continues until either a matching variable declaration can be found, or the global scope is reached and there's nowhere else to go.

It's important to note that compilation doesn't actually *do anything* in terms of reserving memory for scopes and variables. None of the program has been executed yet.

Instead, compilation creates a map of all the lexical scopes that lays out what the program will need while it executes. You can think of this plan as inserted code for use at runtime, which defines all the scopes (aka, "lexical environments") and registers all the identifiers (variables) for each scope.

In other words, while scopes are identified during compilation, they're not actually created until runtime, each time a scope needs to run. In the next chapter, we'll sketch out the conceptual foundations for lexical scope.

Chapter 2: Illustrating Lexical Scope

In Chapter 1, we explored how scope is determined during code compilation, a model called "lexical scope." The term "lexical" refers to the first stage of compilation (lexing/parsing).

To properly *reason* about our programs, it's important to have a solid conceptual foundation of how scope works. If we rely on guesses and intuition, we may accidentally get the right answers some of the time, but many other times we're far off. This isn't a recipe for success.

Like way back in grade school math class, getting the right answer isn't enough if we don't show the correct steps to get there! We need to build accurate and helpful mental models as foundation moving forward.

This chapter will illustrate *scope* with several metaphors. The goal here is to *think* about how your program is handled by the JS engine in ways that more closely align with how the JS engine actually works.

Marbles, and Buckets, and Bubbles... Oh My!

One metaphor I've found effective in understanding scope is sorting colored marbles into buckets of their matching color.

Imagine you come across a pile of marbles, and notice that all the marbles are colored red, blue, or green. Let's sort all the marbles, dropping the red ones into a red bucket, green into a green bucket, and blue into a blue bucket. After sorting, when you later need a green marble, you already know the green bucket is where to go to get it.

In this metaphor, the marbles are the variables in our program. The buckets are scopes (functions and blocks), which we just conceptually assign individual colors for our discussion purposes. The color of each marble is thus determined by which *color* scope we find the marble originally created in.

Let's annotate the running program example from Chapter 1 with scope color labels:

```
// outer/global scope: RED

var students = [
    { id: 14, name: "Kyle" },
    { id: 73, name: "Suzy" },
    { id: 112, name: "Frank" },
    { id: 6, name: "Sarah" }
];

function getStudentName(studentID) {
    // function scope: BLUE

    for (let student of students) {
        // loop scope: GREEN

        if (student.id == studentID) {
            return student.name;
        }
    }
}
```

```
var nextStudent = getStudentName(73);
console.log(nextStudent);    // Suzy
```

We've designated three scope colors with code comments: RED (outermost global scope), BLUE (scope of function `getStudentName(..)`), and GREEN (scope of/inside the `for` loop). But it still may be difficult to recognize the boundaries of these scope buckets when looking at a code listing.

Figure 2 helps visualize the boundaries of the scopes by drawing colored bubbles (aka, buckets) around each:

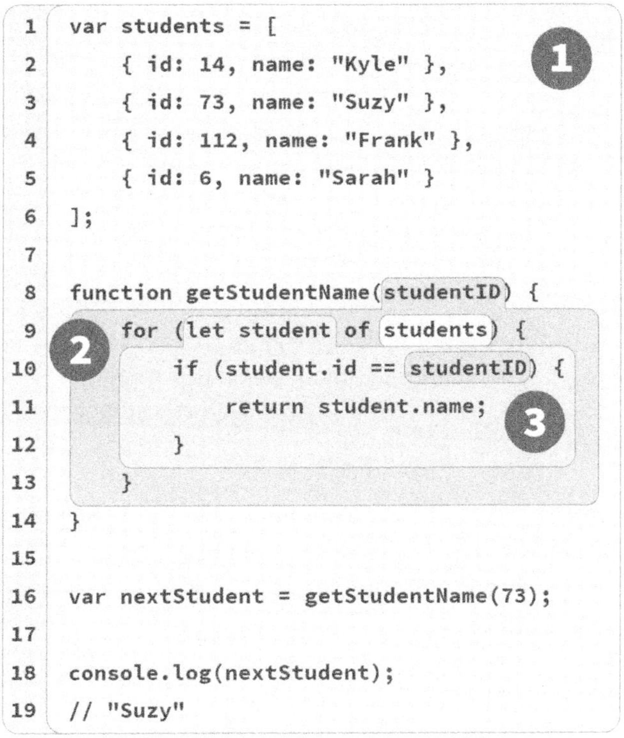
var students = [
{ id: 14, name: "Kyle" },
{ id: 73, name: "Suzy" },
{ id: 112, name: "Frank" },
{ id: 6, name: "Sarah" }
];
function getStudentName(studentID) {
for (let student of students) {
if (student.id == studentID) {
return student.name;
}
}
}
var nextStudent = getStudentName(73);
console.log(nextStudent);
// "Suzy"
1
2
3

Fig. 2: Colored Scope Bubbles

1. **Bubble 1** (RED) encompasses the global scope, which holds three identifiers/variables: `students` (line 1), `getStudentName` (line 8), and `nextStudent` (line 16).
2. **Bubble 2** (BLUE) encompasses the scope of the function `getStudentName(..)` (line 8), which holds just one identifier/variable: the parameter `studentID` (line 8).
3. **Bubble 3** (GREEN) encompasses the scope of the `for`-loop (line 9), which holds just one identifier/variable: `student` (line 9).

> **Note**
>
> Technically, the parameter `studentID` is not exactly in the BLUE(2) scope. We'll unwind that confusion in "Implied Scopes" in Appendix A. For now, it's close enough to label `studentID` a BLUE(2) marble.

Scope bubbles are determined during compilation based on where the functions/blocks of scope are written, the nesting inside each other, and so on. Each scope bubble is entirely contained within its parent scope bubble—a scope is never partially in two different outer scopes.

Each marble (variable/identifier) is colored based on which bubble (bucket) it's declared in, not the color of the scope it may be accessed from (e.g., `students` on line 9 and `studentID` on line 10).

> **Note**
>
> Remember we asserted in Chapter 1 that `id`, `name`, and `log` are all properties, not variables; in other words, they're not marbles in buckets, so they don't get colored based on any the rules we're discussing in this book. To understand how such property accesses are handled, see the third book in the series, *Objects & Classes.*

As the JS engine processes a program (during compilation), and finds a declaration for a variable, it essentially asks, "Which *color* scope (bubble or bucket) am I currently in?" The variable is designated as that same *color*, meaning it belongs to that bucket/bubble.

The GREEN(3) bucket is wholly nested inside of the BLUE(2) bucket, and similarly the BLUE(2) bucket is wholly nested inside the RED(1) bucket. Scopes can nest inside each other as shown, to any depth of nesting as your program needs.

References (non-declarations) to variables/identifiers are allowed if there's a matching declaration either in the current scope, or any scope above/outside the current scope, but not with declarations from lower/nested scopes.

An expression in the RED(1) bucket only has access to RED(1) marbles, **not** BLUE(2) or GREEN(3). An expression in the BLUE(2) bucket can reference either BLUE(2) or RED(1) marbles, **not** GREEN(3). And an expression in the GREEN(3) bucket has access to RED(1), BLUE(2), and GREEN(3) marbles.

We can conceptualize the process of determining these non-declaration marble colors during runtime as a lookup. Since the `students` variable reference in the `for`-loop statement on line 9 is not a declaration, it has no color. So we ask the current BLUE(2) scope bucket if it has a marble matching that name. Since it doesn't, the lookup continues with the next outer/containing scope: RED(1). The RED(1) bucket has a marble of the name `students`, so the loop-statement's `students` variable reference is determined to be a RED(1) marble.

The `if (student.id == studentID)` statement on line 10 similarly references a GREEN(3) marble named `student` and a BLUE(2) marble `studentID`.

> **Note**
>
> The JS engine doesn't generally determine these marble colors during runtime; the "lookup" here is a rhetorical device to help you understand the concepts. During compilation, most or all variable references will match already-known scope buckets, so their color is already determined, and stored with each marble reference to avoid unnecessary lookups as the program runs. More on this nuance in Chapter 3.

The key take-aways from marbles & buckets (and bubbles!):

- Variables are declared in specific scopes, which can be thought of as colored marbles from matching-color buckets.
- Any variable reference that appears in the scope where it was declared, or appears in any deeper nested scopes, will be labeled a marble of that same color—unless an intervening scope "shadows" the variable declaration; see "Shadowing" in Chapter 3.

- The determination of colored buckets, and the marbles they contain, happens during compilation. This information is used for variable (marble color) "lookups" during code execution.

A Conversation Among Friends

Another useful metaphor for the process of analyzing variables and the scopes they come from is to imagine various conversations that occur inside the engine as code is processed and then executed. We can "listen in" on these conversations to get a better conceptual foundation for how scopes work.

Let's now meet the members of the JS engine that will have conversations as they process our program:

- *Engine*: responsible for start-to-finish compilation and execution of our JavaScript program.
- *Compiler*: one of *Engine*'s friends; handles all the dirty work of parsing and code-generation (see previous section).
- *Scope Manager*: another friend of *Engine*; collects and maintains a lookup list of all the declared variables/identifiers, and enforces a set of rules as to how these are accessible to currently executing code.

For you to *fully understand* how JavaScript works, you need to begin to *think* like *Engine* (and friends) think, ask the questions they ask, and answer their questions likewise.

To explore these conversations, recall again our running program example:

```
var students = [
    { id: 14, name: "Kyle" },
    { id: 73, name: "Suzy" },
    { id: 112, name: "Frank" },
    { id: 6, name: "Sarah" }
];

function getStudentName(studentID) {
    for (let student of students) {
        if (student.id == studentID) {
            return student.name;
        }
    }
}

var nextStudent = getStudentName(73);

console.log(nextStudent);
// Suzy
```

Let's examine how JS is going to process that program, specifically starting with the first statement. The array and its contents are just basic JS value literals (and thus unaffected by any scoping concerns), so our focus here will be on the `var students = [ .. ]` declaration and initialization-assignment parts.

We typically think of that as a single statement, but that's not how our friend *Engine* sees it. In fact, JS treats these as two distinct operations, one which *Compiler* will handle during compilation, and the other which *Engine* will handle during execution.

The first thing *Compiler* will do with this program is perform lexing to break it down into tokens, which it will then parse into a tree (AST).

Once *Compiler* gets to code generation, there's more detail to consider than may be obvious. A reasonable assumption would be that *Compiler* will produce code for the first statement such as: "Allocate memory for a variable, label it `students`, then stick a reference to the array into that variable." But that's not the whole story.

Here's the steps *Compiler* will follow to handle that statement:

1. Encountering `var students`, *Compiler* will ask *Scope Manager* to see if a variable named `students` already exists for that particular scope bucket. If so, *Compiler* would ignore this declaration and move on. Otherwise, *Compiler* will produce code that (at execution time) asks *Scope Manager* to create a new variable called `students` in that scope bucket.
2. *Compiler* then produces code for *Engine* to later execute, to handle the `students = []` assignment. The code *Engine* runs will first ask *Scope Manager* if there is a variable called `students` accessible in the current scope bucket. If not, *Engine* keeps looking elsewhere (see "Nested Scope" below). Once *Engine* finds a variable, it assigns the reference of the `[ .. ]` array to it.

In conversational form, the first phase of compilation for the program might play out between *Compiler* and *Scope Manager* like this:

> ***Compiler***: Hey, *Scope Manager* (of the global scope), I found a formal declaration for an identifier called `students`, ever heard of it?

> ***(Global) Scope Manager***: Nope, never heard of it, so I just created it for you.
>
> ***Compiler***: Hey, *Scope Manager*, I found a formal declaration for an identifier called `getStudentName`, ever heard of it?
>
> ***(Global) Scope Manager***: Nope, but I just created it for you.
>
> ***Compiler***: Hey, *Scope Manager*, `getStudentName` points to a function, so we need a new scope bucket.
>
> ***(Function) Scope Manager***: Got it, here's the scope bucket.
>
> ***Compiler***: Hey, *Scope Manager* (of the function), I found a formal parameter declaration for `studentID`, ever heard of it?
>
> ***(Function) Scope Manager***: Nope, but now it's created in this scope.
>
> ***Compiler***: Hey, *Scope Manager* (of the function), I found a `for`-loop that will need its own scope bucket.
>
> ...

The conversation is a question-and-answer exchange, where **Compiler** asks the current *Scope Manager* if an encountered identifier declaration has already been encountered. If "no,"

Scope Manager creates that variable in that scope. If the answer is "yes," then it's effectively skipped over since there's nothing more for that *Scope Manager* to do.

Compiler also signals when it runs across functions or block scopes, so that a new scope bucket and *Scope Manager* can be instantiated.

Later, when it comes to execution of the program, the conversation will shift to *Engine* and *Scope Manager*, and might play out like this:

> ***Engine***: Hey, *Scope Manager* (of the global scope), before we begin, can you look up the identifier `getStudentName` so I can assign this function to it?
>
> ***(Global) Scope Manager***: Yep, here's the variable.
>
> ***Engine***: Hey, *Scope Manager*, I found a *target* reference for `students`, ever heard of it?
>
> ***(Global) Scope Manager***: Yes, it was formally declared for this scope, so here it is.
>
> ***Engine***: Thanks, I'm initializing `students` to `undefined`, so it's ready to use.
>
> Hey, *Scope Manager* (of the global scope), I found a *target* reference for `nextStudent`, ever heard of it?
>
> ***(Global) Scope Manager***: Yes, it was formally declared for this scope, so here it is.

> ***Engine***: Thanks, I'm initializing `nextStudent` to `undefined`, so it's ready to use.
>
> Hey, *Scope Manager* (of the global scope), I found a *source* reference for `getStudentName`, ever heard of it?
>
> ***(Global) Scope Manager***: Yes, it was formally declared for this scope. Here it is.
>
> ***Engine***: Great, the value in `getStudentName` is a function, so I'm going to execute it.
>
> ***Engine***: Hey, *Scope Manager*, now we need to instantiate the function's scope.
>
> ...

This conversation is another question-and-answer exchange, where *Engine* first asks the current *Scope Manager* to look up the hoisted `getStudentName` identifier, so as to associate the function with it. *Engine* then proceeds to ask *Scope Manager* about the *target* reference for `students`, and so on.

To review and summarize how a statement like `var students = [ .. ]` is processed, in two distinct steps:

1. *Compiler* sets up the declaration of the scope variable (since it wasn't previously declared in the current scope).
2. While *Engine* is executing, to process the assignment part of the statement, *Engine* asks *Scope Manager* to look up the variable, initializes it to `undefined` so it's ready to use, and then assigns the array value to it.

Nested Scope

When it comes time to execute the `getStudentName()` function, *Engine* asks for a *Scope Manager* instance for that function's scope, and it will then proceed to look up the parameter (`studentID`) to assign the `73` argument value to, and so on.

The function scope for `getStudentName(..)` is nested inside the global scope. The block scope of the `for`-loop is similarly nested inside that function scope. Scopes can be lexically nested to any arbitrary depth as the program defines.

Each scope gets its own *Scope Manager* instance each time that scope is executed (one or more times). Each scope automatically has all its identifiers registered at the start of the scope being executed (this is called "variable hoisting"; see Chapter 5).

At the beginning of a scope, if any identifier came from a `function` declaration, that variable is automatically initialized to its associated function reference. And if any identifier came from a `var` declaration (as opposed to `let`/`const`), that variable is automatically initialized to `undefined` so that it can be used; otherwise, the variable remains uninitialized (aka, in its "TDZ," see Chapter 5) and cannot be used until its full declaration-and-initialization are executed.

In the `for (let student of students) {` statement, `students` is a *source* reference that must be looked up. But how will that lookup be handled, since the scope of the function will not find such an identifier?

To explain, let's imagine that bit of conversation playing out like this:

> ***Engine***: Hey, *Scope Manager* (for the function), I have a *source* reference for `students`, ever heard of it?
>
> ***(Function) Scope Manager***: Nope, never heard of it. Try the next outer scope.
>
> ***Engine***: Hey, *Scope Manager* (for the global scope), I have a *source* reference for `students`, ever heard of it?
>
> ***(Global) Scope Manager***: Yep, it was formally declared, here it is.
>
> ...

One of the key aspects of lexical scope is that any time an identifier reference cannot be found in the current scope, the next outer scope in the nesting is consulted; that process is repeated until an answer is found or there are no more scopes to consult.

Lookup Failures

When *Engine* exhausts all *lexically available* scopes (moving outward) and still cannot resolve the lookup of an identifier, an error condition then exists. However, depending on the mode of the program (strict-mode or not) and the role of the variable (i.e., *target* vs. *source*; see Chapter 1), this error condition will be handled differently.

Undefined Mess

If the variable is a *source*, an unresolved identifier lookup is considered an undeclared (unknown, missing) variable, which always results in a `ReferenceError` being thrown. Also, if the variable is a *target*, and the code at that moment is running in strict-mode, the variable is considered undeclared and similarly throws a `ReferenceError`.

The error message for an undeclared variable condition, in most JS environments, will look like, "Reference Error: XYZ is not defined." The phrase "not defined" seems almost identical to the word "undefined," as far as the English language goes. But these two are very different in JS, and this error message unfortunately creates a persistent confusion.

"Not defined" really means "not declared"—or, rather, "undeclared," as in a variable that has no matching formal declaration in any *lexically available* scope. By contrast, "undefined" really means a variable was found (declared), but the variable otherwise has no other value in it at the moment, so it defaults to the `undefined` value.

To perpetuate the confusion even further, JS's `typeof` operator returns the string `"undefined"` for variable references in either state:

```
var studentName;
typeof studentName;     // "undefined"

typeof doesntExist;     // "undefined"
```

These two variable references are in very different conditions, but JS sure does muddy the waters. The terminology mess is confusing and terribly unfortunate. Unfortunately, JS developers just have to pay close attention to not mix up *which kind* of "undefined" they're dealing with!

Global... What!?

If the variable is a *target* and strict-mode is not in effect, a confusing and surprising legacy behavior kicks in. The troublesome outcome is that the global scope's *Scope Manager* will just create an **accidental global variable** to fulfill that target assignment!

Consider:

```
function getStudentName() {
    // assignment to an undeclared variable :(
    nextStudent = "Suzy";
}

getStudentName();

console.log(nextStudent);
// "Suzy" -- oops, an accidental-global variable!
```

Here's how that *conversation* will proceed:

> ***Engine***: Hey, *Scope Manager* (for the function), I have a *target* reference for `nextStudent`, ever heard of it?

> ***(Function) Scope Manager***: Nope, never heard of it. Try the next outer scope.

> ***Engine***: Hey, *Scope Manager* (for the global scope), I have a *target* reference for `nextStudent`, ever heard of it?
>
> ***(Global) Scope Manager***: Nope, but since we're in non-strict-mode, I helped you out and just created a global variable for you, here it is!

Yuck.

This sort of accident (almost certain to lead to bugs eventually) is a great example of the beneficial protections offered by strict-mode, and why it's such a bad idea *not* to be using strict-mode. In strict-mode, the ***Global Scope Manager*** would instead have responded:

> ***(Global) Scope Manager***: Nope, never heard of it. Sorry, I've got to throw a `ReferenceError`.

Assigning to a never-declared variable *is* an error, so it's right that we would receive a `ReferenceError` here.

Never rely on accidental global variables. Always use strict-mode, and always formally declare your variables. You'll then get a helpful `ReferenceError` if you ever mistakenly try to assign to a not-declared variable.

Building On Metaphors

To visualize nested scope resolution, I prefer yet another metaphor, an office building, as in Figure 3:

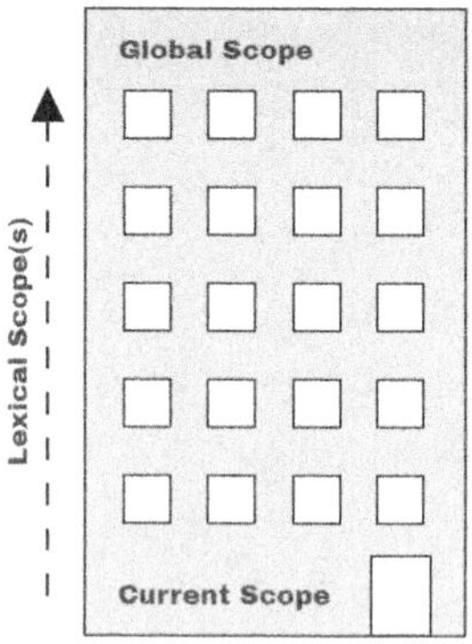

Fig. 3: Scope "Building"

The building represents our program's nested scope collection. The first floor of the building represents the currently executing scope. The top level of the building is the global scope.

You resolve a *target* or *source* variable reference by first looking on the current floor, and if you don't find it, taking the elevator to the next floor (i.e., an outer scope), looking there, then the next, and so on. Once you get to the top floor (the global scope), you either find what you're looking for, or you don't. But you have to stop regardless.

Continue the Conversation

By this point, you should be developing richer mental models for what scope is and how the JS engine determines and uses it from your code.

Before *continuing*, go find some code in one of your projects and run through these conversations. Seriously, actually speak out loud. Find a friend and practice each role with them. If either of you find yourself confused or tripped up, spend more time reviewing this material.

As we move (up) to the next (outer) chapter, we'll explore how the lexical scopes of a program are connected in a chain.

Chapter 3: The Scope Chain

Chapters 1 and 2 laid down a concrete definition of *lexical scope* (and its parts) and illustrated helpful metaphors for its conceptual foundation. Before proceeding with this chapter, find someone else to explain (written or aloud), in your own words, what lexical scope is and why it's useful to understand.

That seems like a step you might skip, but I've found it really does help to take the time to reformulate these ideas as explanations to others. That helps our brains digest what we're learning!

Now it's time to dig into the nuts and bolts, so expect that things will get a lot more detailed from here forward. Stick with it, though, because these discussions really hammer home just how much we all *don't know* about scope, yet. Make sure to take your time with the text and all the code snippets provided.

To refresh the context of our running example, let's recall the color-coded illustration of the nested scope bubbles, from Chapter 2, Figure 2:

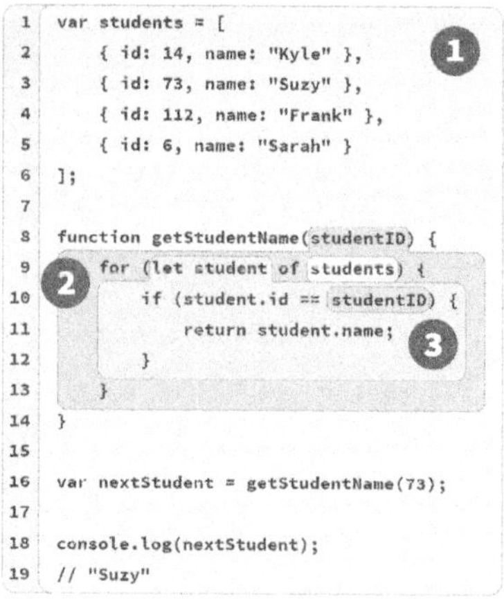
var students = [
{ id: 14, name: "Kyle" },
{ id: 73, name: "Suzy" },
{ id: 112, name: "Frank" },
{ id: 6, name: "Sarah" }
];
function getStudentName(studentID) {
for (let student of students) {
if (student.id == studentID) {
return student.name;
}
}
}
var nextStudent = getStudentName(73);
console.log(nextStudent);
// "Suzy"
1
2
3

Fig. 2 (Ch. 2): Colored Scope Bubbles

The connections between scopes that are nested within other scopes is called the scope chain, which determines the path along which variables can be accessed. The chain is directed, meaning the lookup moves upward/outward only.

"Lookup" Is (Mostly) Conceptual

In Figure 2, notice the color of the `students` variable reference in the `for`-loop. How exactly did we determine that it's a RED(1) marble?

In Chapter 2, we described the runtime access of a variable as a "lookup," where the *Engine* has to start by asking the current scope's *Scope Manager* if it knows about an identifier/variable, and proceeding upward/outward back through the chain of nested scopes (toward the global scope) until found, if ever. The lookup stops as soon as the first matching named declaration in a scope bucket is found.

The lookup process thus determined that `students` is a RED(1) marble, because we had not yet found a matching variable name as we traversed the scope chain, until we arrived at the final RED(1) global scope.

Similarly, `studentID` in the `if`-statement is determined to be a BLUE(2) marble.

This suggestion of a runtime lookup process works well for conceptual understanding, but it's not actually how things usually work in practice.

The color of a marble's bucket (aka, meta information of what scope a variable originates from) is *usually determined* during the initial compilation processing. Because lexical scope is pretty much finalized at that point, a marble's color will not change based on anything that can happen later during runtime.

Since the marble's color is known from compilation, and it's immutable, this information would likely be stored with (or at least accessible from) each variable's entry in the AST; that information is then used explicitly by the executable instructions that constitute the program's runtime.

In other words, *Engine* (from Chapter 2) doesn't need to lookup through a bunch of scopes to figure out which scope bucket a variable comes from. That information is already known! Avoiding the need for a runtime lookup is a key optimization benefit of lexical scope. The runtime operates more performantly without spending time on all these lookups.

But I said "...usually determined..." just a moment ago, with respect to figuring out a marble's color during compilation. So in what case would it ever *not* be known during compilation?

Consider a reference to a variable that isn't declared in any lexically available scopes in the current file—see *Get Started*, Chapter 1, which asserts that each file is its own separate program from the perspective of JS compilation. If no declaration is found, that's not *necessarily* an error. Another file (program) in the runtime may indeed declare that variable in the shared global scope.

So the ultimate determination of whether the variable was ever appropriately declared in some accessible bucket may need to be deferred to the runtime.

Any reference to a variable that's initially *undeclared* is left as an uncolored marble during that file's compilation; this color cannot be determined until other relevant file(s) have been compiled and the application runtime commences. That deferred lookup will eventually resolve the color to whichever scope the variable is found in (likely the global scope).

However, this lookup would only be needed once per variable at most, since nothing else during runtime could later change that marble's color.

The "Lookup Failures" section in Chapter 2 covers what happens if a marble is ultimately still uncolored at the moment its reference is runtime executed.

Shadowing

"Shadowing" might sound mysterious and a little bit sketchy. But don't worry, it's completely legit!

Our running example for these chapters uses different variable names across the scope boundaries. Since they all have unique names, in a way it wouldn't matter if all of them were just stored in one bucket (like RED(1)).

Where having different lexical scope buckets starts to matter more is when you have two or more variables, each in different scopes, with the same lexical names. A single scope cannot have two or more variables with the same name; such multiple references would be assumed as just one variable.

So if you need to maintain two or more variables of the same name, you must use separate (often nested) scopes. And in that case, it's very relevant how the different scope buckets are laid out.

Consider:

```
var studentName = "Suzy";

function printStudent(studentName) {
    studentName = studentName.toUpperCase();
    console.log(studentName);
}

printStudent("Frank");
// FRANK

printStudent(studentName);
// SUZY

console.log(studentName);
// Suzy
```

Tip

Before you move on, take some time to analyze this code using the various techniques/metaphors we've covered in the book. In particular, make sure to identify the marble/bubble colors in this snippet. It's good practice!

The `studentName` variable on line 1 (the `var studentName = ..` statement) creates a RED(1) marble. The same named variable is declared as a BLUE(2) marble on line 3, the parameter in the `printStudent(..)` function definition.

What color marble will `studentName` be in the `studentName = studentName.toUpperCase()` assignment statement and the `console.log(studentName)` statement? All three `studentName` references will be BLUE(2).

With the conceptual notion of the "lookup," we asserted that it starts with the current scope and works its way outward/upward, stopping as soon as a matching variable is found. The BLUE(2) `studentName` is found right away. The RED(1) `studentName` is never even considered.

This is a key aspect of lexical scope behavior, called *shadowing*. The BLUE(2) `studentName` variable (parameter) shadows the RED(1) `studentName`. So, the parameter is shadowing the (shadowed) global variable. Repeat that sentence to yourself a few times to make sure you have the terminology straight!

That's why the re-assignment of `studentName` affects only the inner (parameter) variable: the BLUE(2) `studentName`, not the global RED(1) `studentName`.

When you choose to shadow a variable from an outer scope, one direct impact is that from that scope inward/downward (through any nested scopes) it's now impossible for any marble to be colored as the shadowed variable—(RED(1), in this case). In other words, any `studentName` identifier reference will correspond to that parameter variable, never the global `studentName` variable. It's lexically impossible to reference the global `studentName` anywhere inside of the `printStudent(..)` function (or from any nested scopes).

Global Unshadowing Trick

Please beware: leveraging the technique I'm about to describe is not very good practice, as it's limited in utility, confusing for readers of your code, and likely to invite bugs to your program. I'm covering it only because you may run across this behavior in existing programs, and understanding what's happening is critical to not getting tripped up.

It *is* possible to access a global variable from a scope where that variable has been shadowed, but not through a typical lexical identifier reference.

In the global scope (RED(1)), `var` declarations and `function` declarations also expose themselves as properties (of the same name as the identifier) on the *global object*—essentially an object representation of the global scope. If you've written JS for a browser environment, you probably recognize the global object as `window`. That's not *entirely* accurate, but it's good enough for our discussion. In the next chapter, we'll explore the global scope/object topic more.

Consider this program, specifically executed as a standalone .js file in a browser environment:

```
var studentName = "Suzy";

function printStudent(studentName) {
    console.log(studentName);
    console.log(window.studentName);
}

printStudent("Frank");
// "Frank"
// "Suzy"
```

Notice the `window.studentName` reference? This expression is accessing the global variable `studentName` as a property on `window` (which we're pretending for now is synonymous with the global object). That's the only way to access a shadowed variable from inside a scope where the shadowing variable is present.

The `window.studentName` is a mirror of the global `studentName` variable, not a separate snapshot copy. Changes to one are still seen from the other, in either direction. You can think of `window.studentName` as a getter/setter that accesses the actual `studentName` variable. As a matter of fact, you can even *add* a variable to the global scope by creating/setting a property on the global object.

Warning

Remember: just because you *can* doesn't mean you *should.* Don't shadow a global variable that you need to access, and conversely, avoid using this trick to access a global variable that you've shadowed. And definitely don't confuse readers of your code by creating global variables as `window` properties instead of with formal declarations!

This little "trick" only works for accessing a global scope variable (not a shadowed variable from a nested scope), and even then, only one that was declared with `var` or `function`.

Other forms of global scope declarations do not create mirrored global object properties:

```
var one = 1;
let notOne = 2;
const notTwo = 3;
class notThree {}

console.log(window.one);        // 1
console.log(window.notOne);     // undefined
console.log(window.notTwo);     // undefined
console.log(window.notThree);   // undefined
```

Variables (no matter how they're declared!) that exist in any other scope than the global scope are completely inaccessible from a scope where they've been shadowed:

```
var special = 42;

function lookingFor(special) {
    // The identifier `special` (parameter) in this
    // scope is shadowed inside keepLooking(), and
    // is thus inaccessible from that scope.

    function keepLooking() {
        var special = 3.141592;
        console.log(special);
        console.log(window.special);
    }

    keepLooking();
}

lookingFor(112358132134);
// 3.141592
// 42
```

The global RED(1) `special` is shadowed by the BLUE(2) `special` (parameter), and the BLUE(2) `special` is itself shadowed by the GREEN(3) `special` inside `keepLooking()`. We can still access the RED(1) `special` using the indirect reference `window.special`. But there's no way for `keepLooking()` to access the BLUE(2) `special` that holds the number `112358132134`.

Copying Is Not Accessing

I've been asked the following "But what about...?" question dozens of times. Consider:

```
var special = 42;

function lookingFor(special) {
    var another = {
        special: special
    };

    function keepLooking() {
        var special = 3.141592;
        console.log(special);
        console.log(another.special);  // Ooo, tricky!
        console.log(window.special);
    }

    keepLooking();
}

lookingFor(112358132134);
// 3.141592
// 112358132134
// 42
```

Oh! So does this `another` object technique disprove my claim that the `special` parameter is "completely inaccessible" from inside `keepLooking()`? No, the claim is still correct.

`special: special` is copying the value of the `special` parameter variable into another container (a property of the same name). Of course, if you put a value in another container, shadowing no longer applies (unless `another` was shadowed, too!). But that doesn't mean we're accessing the parameter `special`; it means we're accessing the copy of the value it had at that moment, by way of *another* container (object property). We cannot reassign the BLUE(2) `special` parameter to a different value from inside `keepLooking()`.

Another "But...!?" you may be about to raise: what if I'd used objects or arrays as the values instead of the numbers (`112358132134`, etc.)? Would us having references to objects instead of copies of primitive values "fix" the inaccessibility?

No. Mutating the contents of the object value via a reference copy is **not** the same thing as lexically accessing the variable itself. We still can't reassign the BLUE(2) `special` parameter.

Illegal Shadowing

Not all combinations of declaration shadowing are allowed. `let` can shadow `var`, but `var` cannot shadow `let`:

```
function something() {
    var special = "JavaScript";

    {
        let special = 42;   // totally fine shadowing

        // ..
    }
}
```

```
function another() {
    // ..

    {
        let special = "JavaScript";

        {
            var special = "JavaScript";
            // ^^^ Syntax Error

            // ..
        }
    }
}
```

Notice in the `another()` function, the inner `var special` declaration is attempting to declare a function-wide `special`, which in and of itself is fine (as shown by the `something()` function).

The syntax error description in this case indicates that `special` has already been defined, but that error message is a little misleading—again, no such error happens in `something()`, as shadowing is generally allowed just fine.

The real reason it's raised as a `SyntaxError` is because the `var` is basically trying to "cross the boundary" of (or hop over) the `let` declaration of the same name, which is not allowed.

That boundary-crossing prohibition effectively stops at each function boundary, so this variant raises no exception:

```
function another() {
    // ..

    {
        let special = "JavaScript";

        ajax("https://some.url",function callback(){
            // totally fine shadowing
            var special = "JavaScript";

            // ..
        });
    }
}
```

Summary: `let` (in an inner scope) can always shadow an outer scope's `var`. `var` (in an inner scope) can only shadow an outer scope's `let` if there is a function boundary in between.

Function Name Scope

As you've seen by now, a `function` declaration looks like this:

```
function askQuestion() {
    // ..
}
```

And as discussed in Chapters 1 and 2, such a `function` declaration will create an identifier in the enclosing scope (in this case, the global scope) named `askQuestion`.

What about this program?

```
var askQuestion = function(){
    // ..
};
```

The same is true for the variable `askQuestion` being created. But since it's a `function` expression—a function definition used as value instead of a standalone declaration—the function itself will not "hoist" (see Chapter 5).

One major difference between `function` declarations and `function` expressions is what happens to the name identifier of the function. Consider a named `function` expression:

```
var askQuestion = function ofTheTeacher(){
    // ..
};
```

We know `askQuestion` ends up in the outer scope. But what about the `ofTheTeacher` identifier? For formal `function` declarations, the name identifier ends up in the outer/enclosing scope, so it may be reasonable to assume that's true here. But `ofTheTeacher` is declared as an identifier **inside the function itself**:

```
var askQuestion = function ofTheTeacher() {
    console.log(ofTheTeacher);
};

askQuestion();
// function ofTheTeacher()...

console.log(ofTheTeacher);
// ReferenceError: ofTheTeacher is not defined
```

Note

Actually, `ofTheTeacher` is not exactly *in the scope of the function*. Appendix A, "Implied Scopes" will explain further.

Not only is `ofTheTeacher` declared inside the function rather than outside, but it's also defined as read-only:

```
var askQuestion = function ofTheTeacher() {
    "use strict";
    ofTheTeacher = 42;   // TypeError

    //..
};

askQuestion();
// TypeError
```

Because we used strict-mode, the assignment failure is reported as a `TypeError`; in non-strict-mode, such an assignment fails silently with no exception.

What about when a `function` expression has no name identifier?

```
var askQuestion = function(){
   // ..
};
```

A `function` expression with a name identifier is referred to as a "named function expression," but one without a name identifier is referred to as an "anonymous function expression." Anonymous function expressions clearly have no name identifier that affects either scope.

Note

We'll discuss named vs. anonymous `function` expressions in much more detail, including what factors affect the decision to use one or the other, in Appendix A.

Arrow Functions

ES6 added an additional `function` expression form to the language, called "arrow functions":

```
var askQuestion = () => {
    // ..
};
```

The `=>` arrow function doesn't require the word `function` to define it. Also, the `( .. )` around the parameter list is optional in some simple cases. Likewise, the `{ .. }` around the function body is optional in some cases. And when the `{ .. }` are omitted, a return value is sent out without using a `return` keyword.

Note

The attractiveness of `=>` arrow functions is often sold as "shorter syntax," and that's claimed to equate to objectively more readable code. This claim is dubious at best, and I believe outright misguided. We'll dig into the "readability" of various function forms in Appendix A.

Arrow functions are lexically anonymous, meaning they have no directly related identifier that references the function. The assignment to `askQuestion` creates an inferred name of "askQuestion", but that's **not the same thing as being non-anonymous**:

```
var askQuestion = () => {
    // ..
};

askQuestion.name;   // askQuestion
```

Arrow functions achieve their syntactic brevity at the expense of having to mentally juggle a bunch of variations for different forms/conditions. Just a few, for example:

```
() => 42;

id => id.toUpperCase();

(id,name) => ({ id, name });

(...args) => {
    return args[args.length - 1];
};
```

The real reason I bring up arrow functions is because of the common but incorrect claim that arrow functions somehow behave differently with respect to lexical scope from standard `function` functions.

This is incorrect.

Other than being anonymous (and having no declarative form), => arrow functions have the same lexical scope rules as `function` functions do. An arrow function, with or without `{ .. }` around its body, still creates a separate, inner nested bucket of scope. Variable declarations inside this nested scope bucket behave the same as in a `function` scope.

Backing Out

When a function (declaration or expression) is defined, a new scope is created. The positioning of scopes nested inside one another creates a natural scope hierarchy throughout the program, called the scope chain. The scope chain controls variable access, directionally oriented upward and outward.

Each new scope offers a clean slate, a space to hold its own set of variables. When a variable name is repeated at different levels of the scope chain, shadowing occurs, which prevents access to the outer variable from that point inward.

As we step back out from these finer details, the next chapter shifts focus to the primary scope all JS programs include: the global scope.

Chapter 4: Around the Global Scope

Chapter 3 mentioned the "global scope" several times, but you may still be wondering why a program's outermost scope is all that important in modern JS. The vast majority of work is now done inside of functions and modules rather than globally.

Is it good enough to just assert, "Avoid using the global scope," and be done with it?

The global scope of a JS program is a rich topic, with much more utility and nuance than you would likely assume. This chapter first explores how the global scope is (still) useful and relevant to writing JS programs today, then looks at differences in where and *how to access* the global scope in different JS environments.

Fully understanding the global scope is critical in your mastery of using lexical scope to structure your programs.

Why Global Scope?

It's likely no surprise to readers that most applications are composed of multiple (sometimes many!) individual JS files. So how exactly do all those separate files get stitched together in a single runtime context by the JS engine?

With respect to browser-executed applications, there are three main ways.

First, if you're directly using ES modules (not transpiling them into some other module-bundle format), these files are loaded individually by the JS environment. Each module then `imports` references to whichever other modules it needs to access. The separate module files cooperate with each other exclusively through these shared imports, without needing any shared outer scope.

Second, if you're using a bundler in your build process, all the files are typically concatenated together before delivery to the browser and JS engine, which then only processes one big file. Even with all the pieces of the application co-located in a single file, some mechanism is necessary for each piece to register a *name* to be referred to by other pieces, as well as some facility for that access to occur.

In some build setups, the entire contents of the file are wrapped in a single enclosing scope, such as a wrapper function, universal module (UMD—see Appendix A), etc. Each piece can register itself for access from other pieces by way of local variables in that shared scope. For example:

```
(function wrappingOuterScope(){
    var moduleOne = (function one(){
        // ..
    })();

    var moduleTwo = (function two(){
        // ..

        function callModuleOne() {
            moduleOne.someMethod();
        }
```

```
        // ..
    })();
})();
```

As shown, the `moduleOne` and `moduleTwo` local variables inside the `wrappingOuterScope()` function scope are declared so that these modules can access each other for their cooperation.

While the scope of `wrappingOuterScope()` is a function and not the full environment global scope, it does act as a sort of "application-wide scope," a bucket where all the top-level identifiers can be stored, though not in the real global scope. It's kind of like a stand-in for the global scope in that respect.

And finally, the third way: whether a bundler tool is used for an application, or whether the (non-ES module) files are simply loaded in the browser individually (via `<script>` tags or other dynamic JS resource loading), if there is no single surrounding scope encompassing all these pieces, the **global scope** is the only way for them to cooperate with each other:

A bundled file of this sort often looks something like this:

```
var moduleOne = (function one(){
    // ..
})();
var moduleTwo = (function two(){
    // ..

    function callModuleOne() {
        moduleOne.someMethod();
    }

    // ..
})();
```

Here, since there is no surrounding function scope, these `moduleOne` and `moduleTwo` declarations are simply dropped into the global scope. This is effectively the same as if the files hadn't been concatenated, but loaded separately:

module1.js:

```
var moduleOne = (function one(){
    // ..
})();
```

module2.js:

```
var moduleTwo = (function two(){
    // ..

    function callModuleOne() {
        moduleOne.someMethod();
    }

    // ..
})();
```

If these files are loaded separately as normal standalone .js files in a browser environment, each top-level variable declaration will end up as a global variable, since the global scope is the only shared resource between these two separate files—they're independent programs, from the perspective of the JS engine.

In addition to (potentially) accounting for where an application's code resides during runtime, and how each piece is able to access the other pieces to cooperate, the global scope is also where:

- JS exposes its built-ins:
  - primitives: `undefined`, `null`, `Infinity`, `NaN`
  - natives: `Date()`, `Object()`, `String()`, etc.
  - global functions: `eval()`, `parseInt()`, etc.
  - namespaces: `Math`, `Atomics`, `JSON`
  - friends of JS: `Intl`, `WebAssembly`
- The environment hosting the JS engine exposes its own built-ins:
  - `console` (and its methods)
  - the DOM (`window`, `document`, etc)
  - timers (`setTimeout(..)`, etc)
  - web platform APIs: `navigator`, `history`, geolocation, WebRTC, etc.

These are just some of the many *globals* your programs will interact with.

Note

Node also exposes several elements "globally," but they're technically not in the `global` scope: `require()`, `__dirname`, `module`, `URL`, and so on.

Most developers agree that the global scope shouldn't just be a dumping ground for every variable in your application. That's a mess of bugs just waiting to happen. But it's also undeniable that the global scope is an important *glue* for practically every JS application.

Where Exactly is this Global Scope?

It might seem obvious that the global scope is located in the outermost portion of a file; that is, not inside any function or other block. But it's not quite as simple as that.

Different JS environments handle the scopes of your programs, especially the global scope, differently. It's quite common for JS developers to harbor misconceptions without even realizing it.

Browser "Window"

With respect to treatment of the global scope, the most *pure* environment JS can be run in is as a standalone .js file loaded in a web page environment in a browser. I don't mean "pure" as in nothing automatically added—lots may be added!—but rather in terms of minimal intrusion on the code or interference with its expected global scope behavior.

Consider this .js file:

```
var studentName = "Kyle";

function hello() {
    console.log(`Hello, ${ studentName }!`);
}

hello();
// Hello, Kyle!
```

This code may be loaded in a web page environment using an inline `<script>` tag, a `<script src=..>` script tag in the markup, or even a dynamically created `<script>` DOM element. In all three cases, the `studentName` and `hello` identifiers are declared in the global scope.

That means if you access the global object (commonly, `window` in the browser), you'll find properties of those same names there:

```
var studentName = "Kyle";

function hello() {
    console.log(`Hello, ${ window.studentName }!`);
}

window.hello();
// Hello, Kyle!
```

That's the default behavior one would expect from a reading of the JS specification: the outer scope *is* the global scope and `studentName` is legitimately created as global variable.

That's what I mean by *pure*. But unfortunately, that won't always be true of all JS environments you encounter, and that's often surprising to JS developers.

Globals Shadowing Globals

Recall the discussion of shadowing (and global unshadowing) from Chapter 3, where one variable declaration can override and prevent access to a declaration of the same name from an outer scope.

An unusual consequence of the difference between a global variable and a global property of the same name is that, within just the global scope itself, a global object property can be shadowed by a global variable:

```
window.something = 42;

let something = "Kyle";

console.log(something);
// Kyle

console.log(window.something);
// 42
```

The `let` declaration adds a `something` global variable but not a global object property (see Chapter 3). The effect then is that the `something` lexical identifier shadows the `something` global object property.

It's almost certainly a bad idea to create a divergence between the global object and the global scope. Readers of your code will almost certainly be tripped up.

A simple way to avoid this gotcha with global declarations: always use `var` for globals. Reserve `let` and `const` for block scopes (see "Scoping with Blocks" in Chapter 6).

DOM Globals

I asserted that a browser-hosted JS environment has the most *pure* global scope behavior we'll see. However, it's not entirely *pure*.

One surprising behavior in the global scope you may encounter with browser-based JS applications: a DOM element with an `id` attribute automatically creates a global variable that references it.

Consider this markup:

```
<ul id="my-todo-list">
   <li id="first">Write a book</li>
   ..
</ul>
```

And the JS for that page could include:

```
first;
// <li id="first">..</li>

window["my-todo-list"];
// <ul id="my-todo-list">..</ul>
```

If the `id` value is a valid lexical name (like `first`), the lexical variable is created. If not, the only way to access that global is through the global object (`window[..]`).

The auto-registration of all `id`-bearing DOM elements as global variables is an old legacy browser behavior that nevertheless must remain because so many old sites still rely on it. My advice is never to use these global variables, even though they will always be silently created.

What's in a (Window) Name?

Another global scope oddity in browser-based JS:

```
var name = 42;

console.log(name, typeof name);
// "42" string
```

`window.name` is a pre-defined "global" in a browser context; it's a property on the global object, so it seems like a normal global variable (yet it's anything but "normal").

We used `var` for our declaration, which **does not** shadow the pre-defined `name` global property. That means, effectively, the `var` declaration is ignored, since there's already a global scope object property of that name. As we discussed earlier, had we used `let name`, we would have shadowed `window.name` with a separate global `name` variable.

But the truly surprising behavior is that even though we assigned the number `42` to `name` (and thus `window.name`), when we then retrieve its value, it's a string `"42"`! In this case, the weirdness is because `name` is actually a pre-defined getter/setter on the `window` object, which insists on its value being a string value. Yikes!

With the exception of some rare corner cases like DOM element ID's and `window.name`, JS running as a standalone file in a browser page has some of the most *pure* global scope behavior we will encounter.

Web Workers

Web Workers are a web platform extension on top of browser-JS behavior, which allows a JS file to run in a completely separate thread (operating system wise) from the thread that's running the main JS program.

Since these Web Worker programs run on a separate thread, they're restricted in their communications with the main application thread, to avoid/limit race conditions and other complications. Web Worker code does not have access to the DOM, for example. Some web APIs are, however, made available to the worker, such as `navigator`.

Since a Web Worker is treated as a wholly separate program, it does not share the global scope with the main JS program.

However, the browser's JS engine is still running the code, so we can expect similar *purity* of its global scope behavior. Since there is no DOM access, the `window` alias for the global scope doesn't exist.

In a Web Worker, the global object reference is typically made using `self`:

```
var studentName = "Kyle";
let studentID = 42;

function hello() {
    console.log(`Hello, ${ self.studentName }!`);
}

self.hello();
// Hello, Kyle!

self.studentID;
// undefined
```

Just as with main JS programs, `var` and `function` declarations create mirrored properties on the global object (aka, `self`), where other declarations (`let`, etc) do not.

So again, the global scope behavior we're seeing here is about as *pure* as it gets for running JS programs; perhaps it's even more *pure* since there's no DOM to muck things up!

Developer Tools Console/REPL

Recall from Chapter 1 in *Get Started* that Developer Tools don't create a completely adherent JS environment. They do process JS code, but they also lean in favor of the UX interaction being most friendly to developers (aka, developer experience, or DX).

In some cases, favoring DX when typing in short JS snippets, over the normal strict steps expected for processing a full JS program, produces observable differences in code behavior between programs and tools. For example, certain error conditions applicable to a JS program may be relaxed and not displayed when the code is entered into a developer tool.

With respect to our discussions here about scope, such observable differences in behavior may include:

- The behavior of the global scope
- Hoisting (see Chapter 5)
- Block-scoping declarators (`let` / `const`, see Chapter 6) when used in the outermost scope

Although it might seem, while using the console/REPL, that statements entered in the outermost scope are being processed in the real global scope, that's not quite accurate. Such tools typically emulate the global scope position to an extent; it's emulation, not strict adherence. These tool environments prioritize developer convenience, which means that at times (such as with our current discussions regarding scope), observed behavior may deviate from the JS specification.

The take-away is that Developer Tools, while optimized to be convenient and useful for a variety of developer activities, are **not** suitable environments to determine or verify explicit and nuanced behaviors of an actual JS program context.

ES Modules (ESM)

ES6 introduced first-class support for the module pattern (covered in Chapter 8). One of the most obvious impacts of using ESM is how it changes the behavior of the observably top-level scope in a file.

Recall this code snippet from earlier (which we'll adjust to ESM format by using the `export` keyword):

```
var studentName = "Kyle";

function hello() {
    console.log(`Hello, ${ studentName }!`);
}

hello();
// Hello, Kyle!

export hello;
```

If that code is in a file that's loaded as an ES module, it will still run exactly the same. However, the observable effects, from the overall application perspective, will be different.

Despite being declared at the top level of the (module) file, in the outermost obvious scope, `studentName` and `hello` are not global variables. Instead, they are module-wide, or if you prefer, "module-global."

However, in a module there's no implicit "module-wide scope object" for these top-level declarations to be added to as properties, as there is when declarations appear in the top-level of non-module JS files. This is not to say that global variables cannot exist or be accessed in such programs. It's just that global variables don't get *created* by declaring variables in the top-level scope of a module.

The module's top-level scope is descended from the global scope, almost as if the entire contents of the module were wrapped in a function. Thus, all variables that exist in the global scope (whether they're on the global object or not!) are available as lexical identifiers from inside the module's scope.

ESM encourages a minimization of reliance on the global scope, where you import whatever modules you may need for the current module to operate. As such, you less often see usage of the global scope or its global object.

However, as noted earlier, there are still plenty of JS and web globals that you will continue to access from the global scope, whether you realize it or not!

Node

One aspect of Node that often catches JS developers off-guard is that Node treats every single .js file that it loads, including the main one you start the Node process with, as a *module* (ES module or CommonJS module, see Chapter 8). The practical effect is that the top level of your Node programs **is never actually the global scope**, the way it is when loading a non-module file in the browser.

As of time of this writing, Node has recently added support for ES modules. But additionally, Node has from its beginning supported a module format referred to as "CommonJS", which looks like this:

```
var studentName = "Kyle";

function hello() {
    console.log(`Hello, ${ studentName }!`);
}

hello();
// Hello, Kyle!

module.exports.hello = hello;
```

Before processing, Node effectively wraps such code in a function, so that the `var` and `function` declarations are contained in that wrapping function's scope, **not** treated as global variables.

Envision the preceding code as being seen by Node as this (illustrative, not actual):

```
function Module(module,require,__dirname,...) {
    var studentName = "Kyle";

    function hello() {
        console.log(`Hello, ${ studentName }!`);
    }

    hello();
    // Hello, Kyle!

    module.exports.hello = hello;
}
```

Node then essentially invokes the added `Module(..)` function to run your module. You can clearly see here why `studentName` and `hello` identifiers are not global, but rather declared in the module scope.

As noted earlier, Node defines a number of "globals" like `require()`, but they're not actually identifiers in the global scope (nor properties of the global object). They're injected in the scope of every module, essentially a bit like the parameters listed in the `Module(..)` function declaration.

So how do you define actual global variables in Node? The only way to do so is to add properties to another of Node's automatically provided "globals," which is ironically called `global`. `global` is a reference to the real global scope object, somewhat like using `window` in a browser JS environment.

Consider:

```
global.studentName = "Kyle";

function hello() {
    console.log(`Hello, ${ studentName }!`);
}

hello();
// Hello, Kyle!

module.exports.hello = hello;
```

Here we add `studentName` as a property on the `global` object, and then in the `console.log(..)` statement we're able to access `studentName` as a normal global variable.

Remember, the identifier `global` is not defined by JS; it's specifically defined by Node.

Global This

Reviewing the JS environments we've looked at so far, a program may or may not:

- Declare a global variable in the top-level scope with `var` or `function` declarations—or `let`, `const`, and `class`.
- Also add global variables declarations as properties of the global scope object if `var` or `function` are used for the declaration.
- Refer to the global scope object (for adding or retrieving global variables, as properties) with `window`, `self`, or `global`.

I think it's fair to say that global scope access and behavior is more complicated than most developers assume, as the preceding sections have illustrated. But the complexity is never more obvious than in trying to nail down a universally applicable reference to the global scope object.

Yet another "trick" for obtaining a reference to the global scope object looks like:

```
const theGlobalScopeObject =
    (new Function("return this"))();
```

Note

A function can be dynamically constructed from code stored in a string value with the `Function()` constructor, similar to `eval(..)` (see "Cheating: Runtime Scope Modifications" in Chapter 1). Such a function will automatically be run in non-strict-mode (for legacy reasons) when invoked with the normal `()` function invocation as shown; its `this` will point at the global object. See the third book in the series, *Objects & Classes*, for more information on determining `this` bindings.

So, we have `window`, `self`, `global`, and this ugly `new Function(..)` trick. That's a lot of different ways to try to get at this global object. Each has its pros and cons.

Why not introduce yet another!?!?

As of ES2020, JS has finally defined a standardized reference to the global scope object, called `globalThis`. So, subject to the recency of the JS engines your code runs in, you can use `globalThis` in place of any of those other approaches.

We could even attempt to define a cross-environment polyfill that's safer across pre-`globalThis` JS environments, such as:

```
const theGlobalScopeObject =
    (typeof globalThis != "undefined") ? globalThis :
    (typeof global != "undefined") ? global :
    (typeof window != "undefined") ? window :
    (typeof self != "undefined") ? self :
    (new Function("return this"))();
```

Phew! That's certainly not ideal, but it works if you find yourself needing a reliable global scope reference.

(The proposed name `globalThis` was fairly controversial while the feature was being added to JS. Specifically, I and many others felt the "this" reference in its name was misleading, since the reason you reference this object is to access to the global scope, never to access some sort of global/default `this` binding. There were many other names considered, but for a variety of reasons ruled out. Unfortunately, the name chosen ended up as a last resort. If you plan to interact with the global scope object in your programs, to reduce confusion, I strongly recommend choosing a better name, such as (the laughably long but accurate!) `theGlobalScopeObject` used here.)

Globally Aware

The global scope is present and relevant in every JS program, even though modern patterns for organizing code into modules de-emphasizes much of the reliance on storing identifiers in that namespace.

Still, as our code proliferates more and more beyond the confines of the browser, it's especially important we have a solid grasp on the differences in how the global scope (and global scope object!) behave across different JS environments.

With the big picture of global scope now sharper in focus, the next chapter again descends into the deeper details of lexical scope, examining how and when variables can be used.

Chapter 5: The (Not So) Secret Lifecycle of Variables

By now you should have a decent grasp of the nesting of scopes, from the global scope downward—called a program's scope chain.

But just knowing which scope a variable comes from is only part of the story. If a variable declaration appears past the first statement of a scope, how will any references to that identifier *before* the declaration behave? What happens if you try to declare the same variable twice in a scope?

JS's particular flavor of lexical scope is rich with nuance in how and when variables come into existence and become available to the program.

When Can I Use a Variable?

At what point does a variable become available to use within its scope? There may seem to be an obvious answer: *after* the variable has been declared/created. Right? Not quite.

Consider:

```
greeting();
// Hello!

function greeting() {
    console.log("Hello!");
}
```

This code works fine. You may have seen or even written code like it before. But did you ever wonder how or why it works? Specifically, why can you access the identifier `greeting` from line 1 (to retrieve and execute a function reference), even though the `greeting()` function declaration doesn't occur until line 4?

Recall Chapter 1 points out that all identifiers are registered to their respective scopes during compile time. Moreover, every identifier is *created* at the beginning of the scope it belongs to, **every time that scope is entered**.

The term most commonly used for a variable being visible from the beginning of its enclosing scope, even though its declaration may appear further down in the scope, is called **hoisting**.

But hoisting alone doesn't fully answer the question. We can see an identifier called `greeting` from the beginning of the scope, but why can we **call** the `greeting()` function before it's been declared?

In other words, how does the variable `greeting` have any value (the function reference) assigned to it, from the moment the scope starts running? The answer is a special characteristic of formal `function` declarations, called *function hoisting*. When a `function` declaration's name identifier is registered at the top of its scope, it's additionally auto-initialized to that function's reference. That's why the function can be called throughout the entire scope!

One key detail is that both *function hoisting* and `var`-flavored *variable hoisting* attach their name identifiers to the nearest enclosing **function scope** (or, if none, the global scope), not a block scope.

> **Note**
>
> Declarations with `let` and `const` still hoist (see the TDZ discussion later in this chapter). But these two declaration forms attach to their enclosing block rather than just an enclosing function as with `var` and `function` declarations. See "Scoping with Blocks" in Chapter 6 for more information.

Hoisting: Declaration vs. Expression

Function hoisting only applies to formal `function` declarations (specifically those which appear outside of blocks—see "FiB" in Chapter 6), not to `function` expression assignments. Consider:

```
greeting();
// TypeError

var greeting = function greeting() {
    console.log("Hello!");
};
```

Line 1 (`greeting();`) throws an error. But the *kind* of error thrown is very important to notice. A `TypeError` means we're trying to do something with a value that is not allowed. Depending on your JS environment, the error message would say something like, "'undefined' is not a function," or more helpfully, "'greeting' is not a function."

Notice that the error is **not** a `ReferenceError`. JS isn't telling us that it couldn't find `greeting` as an identifier in the scope. It's telling us that `greeting` was found but doesn't hold a function reference at that moment. Only functions can be invoked, so attempting to invoke some non-function value results in an error.

But what does `greeting` hold, if not the function reference?

In addition to being hoisted, variables declared with `var` are also automatically initialized to `undefined` at the beginning of their scope—again, the nearest enclosing function, or the global. Once initialized, they're available to be used (assigned to, retrieved from, etc.) throughout the whole scope.

So on that first line, `greeting` exists, but it holds only the default `undefined` value. It's not until line 4 that `greeting` gets assigned the function reference.

Pay close attention to the distinction here. A `function` declaration is hoisted **and initialized to its function value** (again, called *function hoisting*). A `var` variable is also hoisted, and then auto-initialized to `undefined`. Any subsequent `function` expression assignments to that variable don't happen until that assignment is processed during runtime execution.

In both cases, the name of the identifier is hoisted. But the function reference association isn't handled at initialization time (beginning of the scope) unless the identifier was created in a formal `function` declaration.

Variable Hoisting

Let's look at another example of *variable hoisting*:

```
greeting = "Hello!";
console.log(greeting);
// Hello!

var greeting = "Howdy!";
```

Though `greeting` isn't declared until line 5, it's available to be assigned to as early as line 1. Why?

There's two necessary parts to the explanation:

- the identifier is hoisted,
- **and** it's automatically initialized to the value `undefined` from the top of the scope.

> **Note**
>
> Using *variable hoisting* of this sort probably feels unnatural, and many readers might rightly want to avoid relying on it in their programs. But should all hoisting (including *function hoisting*) be avoided? We'll explore these different perspectives on hoisting in more detail in Appendix A.

Hoisting: Yet Another Metaphor

Chapter 2 was full of metaphors (to illustrate scope), but here we are faced with yet another: hoisting itself. Rather than hoisting being a concrete execution step the JS engine performs, it's more useful to think of hoisting as a visualization of various actions JS takes in setting up the program **before execution**.

The typical assertion of what hoisting means: *lifting*—like lifting a heavy weight upward—any identifiers all the way to the top of a scope. The explanation often asserted is that the JS engine will actually *rewrite* that program before execution, so that it looks more like this:

```
var greeting;               // hoisted declaration
greeting = "Hello!";        // the original line 1
console.log(greeting);      // Hello!
greeting = "Howdy!";        // `var` is gone!
```

The hoisting (metaphor) proposes that JS pre-processes the original program and re-arranges it a bit, so that all the declarations have been moved to the top of their respective scopes, before execution. Moreover, the hoisting metaphor asserts that `function` declarations are, in their entirety, hoisted to the top of each scope. Consider:

```
studentName = "Suzy";
greeting();
// Hello Suzy!

function greeting() {
    console.log(`Hello ${ studentName }!`);
}
var studentName;
```

The "rule" of the hoisting metaphor is that function declarations are hoisted first, then variables are hoisted immediately after all the functions. Thus, the hoisting story suggests that program is *re-arranged* by the JS engine to look like this:

```
function greeting() {
    console.log(`Hello ${ studentName }!`);
}
var studentName;

studentName = "Suzy";
greeting();
// Hello Suzy!
```

This hoisting metaphor is convenient. Its benefit is allowing us to hand wave over the magical look-ahead pre-processing necessary to find all these declarations buried deep in scopes and somehow move (hoist) them to the top; we can just think about the program as if it's executed by the JS engine in a **single pass**, top-down.

Single-pass definitely seems more straightforward than Chapter 1's assertion of a two-phase processing.

Hoisting as a mechanism for re-ordering code may be an attractive simplification, but it's not accurate. The JS engine doesn't actually re-arrange the code. It can't magically look ahead and find declarations; the only way to accurately find them, as well as all the scope boundaries in the program, would be to fully parse the code.

Guess what parsing is? The first phase of the two-phase processing! There's no magical mental gymnastics that gets around that fact.

So if the hoisting metaphor is (at best) inaccurate, what should we do with the term? I think it's still useful—indeed, even members of TC39 regularly use it!—but I don't think we should claim it's an actual re-arrangement of source code.

> **Warning**
>
> Incorrect or incomplete mental models often still seem sufficient because they can occasionally lead to accidental right answers. But in the long run it's harder to accurately analyze and predict outcomes if your thinking isn't particularly aligned with how the JS engine works.

I assert that hoisting *should* be used to refer to the **compile-time operation** of generating runtime instructions for the automatic registration of a variable at the beginning of its scope, each time that scope is entered.

That's a subtle but important shift, from hoisting as a runtime behavior to its proper place among compile-time tasks.

Re-declaration?

What do you think happens when a variable is declared more than once in the same scope? Consider:

```
var studentName = "Frank";
console.log(studentName);
// Frank

var studentName;
console.log(studentName);   // ???
```

What do you expect to be printed for that second message? Many believe the second `var studentName` has re-declared the variable (and thus "reset" it), so they expect `undefined` to be printed.

But is there such a thing as a variable being "re-declared" in the same scope? No.

If you consider this program from the perspective of the hoisting metaphor, the code would be re-arranged like this for execution purposes:

```
var studentName;
var studentName;    // clearly a pointless no-op!

studentName = "Frank";
console.log(studentName);
// Frank

console.log(studentName);
// Frank
```

Since hoisting is actually about registering a variable at the beginning of a scope, there's nothing to be done in the middle of the scope where the original program actually had the second `var studentName` statement. It's just a no-op(eration), a pointless statement.

Tip

In the style of the conversation narrative from Chapter 2, *Compiler* would find the second `var` declaration statement and ask the *Scope Manager* if it had already seen a `studentName` identifier; since it had, there wouldn't be anything else to do.

It's also important to point out that `var studentName;` doesn't mean `var studentName = undefined;`, as most assume. Let's prove they're different by considering this variation of the program:

```
var studentName = "Frank";
console.log(studentName);   // Frank

var studentName;
console.log(studentName);   // Frank <--- still!

// let's add the initialization explicitly
var studentName = undefined;
console.log(studentName);   // undefined <--- see!?
```

See how the explicit `= undefined` initialization produces a different outcome than assuming it happens implicitly when omitted? In the next section, we'll revisit this topic of initialization of variables from their declarations.

A repeated `var` declaration of the same identifier name in a scope is effectively a do-nothing operation. Here's another illustration, this time across a function of the same name:

```
var greeting;

function greeting() {
    console.log("Hello!");
}

// basically, a no-op
var greeting;

typeof greeting;        // "function"
```

```
var greeting = "Hello!";

typeof greeting;        // "string"
```

The first `greeting` declaration registers the identifier to the scope, and because it's a `var` the auto-initialization will be `undefined`. The `function` declaration doesn't need to re-register the identifier, but because of *function hoisting* it overrides the auto-initialization to use the function reference. The second `var greeting` by itself doesn't do anything since `greeting` is already an identifier and *function hoisting* already took precedence for the auto-initialization.

Actually assigning `"Hello!"` to `greeting` changes its value from the initial function `greeting()` to the string; `var` itself doesn't have any effect.

What about repeating a declaration within a scope using `let` or `const`?

```
let studentName = "Frank";

console.log(studentName);

let studentName = "Suzy";
```

This program will not execute, but instead immediately throw a `SyntaxError`. Depending on your JS environment, the error message will indicate something like: "studentName has already been declared." In other words, this is a case where attempted "re-declaration" is explicitly not allowed!

It's not just that two declarations involving `let` will throw this error. If either declaration uses `let`, the other can be either `let` or `var`, and the error will still occur, as illustrated with these two variations:

```
var studentName = "Frank";

let studentName = "Suzy";
```

and:

```
let studentName = "Frank";

var studentName = "Suzy";
```

In both cases, a `SyntaxError` is thrown on the *second* declaration. In other words, the only way to "re-declare" a variable is to use `var` for all (two or more) of its declarations.

But why disallow it? The reason for the error is not technical per se, as `var` "re-declaration" has always been allowed; clearly, the same allowance could have been made for `let`.

It's really more of a "social engineering" issue. "Re-declaration" of variables is seen by some, including many on the TC39 body, as a bad habit that can lead to program bugs. So when ES6 introduced `let`, they decided to prevent "re-declaration" with an error.

> **Note**
>
> This is of course a stylistic opinion, not really a technical argument. Many developers agree with the position, and that's probably in part why TC39 included the error (as well as `let` conforming to `const`). But a reasonable case could have been made that staying consistent with `var`'s precedent was more prudent, and that such opinion-enforcement was best left to opt-in tooling like linters. In Appendix A, we'll explore whether `var` (and its associated behavior, like "re-declaration") can still be useful in modern JS.

When *Compiler* asks *Scope Manager* about a declaration, if that identifier has already been declared, and if either/both declarations were made with `let`, an error is thrown. The intended signal to the developer is "Stop relying on sloppy re-declaration!"

Constants?

The `const` keyword is more constrained than `let`. Like `let`, `const` cannot be repeated with the same identifier in the same scope. But there's actually an overriding technical reason why that sort of "re-declaration" is disallowed, unlike `let` which disallows "re-declaration" mostly for stylistic reasons.

The `const` keyword requires a variable to be initialized, so omitting an assignment from the declaration results in a `SyntaxError`:

```
const empty;   // SyntaxError
```

`const` declarations create variables that cannot be re-assigned:

```
const studentName = "Frank";
console.log(studentName);
// Frank

studentName = "Suzy";   // TypeError
```

The `studentName` variable cannot be re-assigned because it's declared with a `const`.

> **Warning**
>
> The error thrown when re-assigning `studentName` is a `TypeError`, not a `SyntaxError`. The subtle distinction here is actually pretty important, but unfortunately far too easy to miss. Syntax errors represent faults in the program that stop it from even starting execution. Type errors represent faults that arise during program execution. In the preceding snippet, `"Frank"` is printed out before we process the re-assignment of `studentName`, which then throws the error.

So if `const` declarations cannot be re-assigned, and `const` declarations always require assignments, then we have a clear technical reason why `const` must disallow any "re-declarations": any `const` "re-declaration" would also necessarily be a `const` re-assignment, which can't be allowed!

```
const studentName = "Frank";

// obviously this must be an error
const studentName = "Suzy";
```

Since `const` "re-declaration" must be disallowed (on those technical grounds), TC39 essentially felt that `let` "re-declaration" should be disallowed as well, for consistency. It's debatable if this was the best choice, but at least we have the reasoning behind the decision.

Loops

So it's clear from our previous discussion that JS doesn't really want us to "re-declare" our variables within the same scope.

That probably seems like a straightforward admonition, until you consider what it means for repeated execution of declaration statements in loops. Consider:

```
var keepGoing = true;
while (keepGoing) {
    let value = Math.random();
    if (value > 0.5) {
        keepGoing = false;
    }
}
```

Is `value` being "re-declared" repeatedly in this program? Will we get errors thrown? No.

All the rules of scope (including "re-declaration" of `let`-created variables) are applied *per scope instance*. In other words, each time a scope is entered during execution, everything resets.

Each loop iteration is its own new scope instance, and within each scope instance, `value` is only being declared once. So there's no attempted "re-declaration," and thus no error. Before we consider other loop forms, what if the `value` declaration in the previous snippet were changed to a `var`?

```
var keepGoing = true;
while (keepGoing) {
    var value = Math.random();
    if (value > 0.5) {
        keepGoing = false;
    }
}
```

Is `value` being "re-declared" here, especially since we know `var` allows it? No. Because `var` is not treated as a block-scoping declaration (see Chapter 6), it attaches itself to the global scope. So there's just one `value` variable, in the same scope as `keepGoing` (global scope, in this case). No "re-declaration" here, either!

One way to keep this all straight is to remember that `var`, `let`, and `const` keywords are effectively *removed* from the code by the time it starts to execute. They're handled entirely by the compiler.

If you mentally erase the declarator keywords and then try to process the code, it should help you decide if and when (re-)declarations might occur.

What about "re-declaration" with other loop forms, like `for`-loops?

```
for (let i = 0; i < 3; i++) {
    let value = i * 10;
    console.log(`${ i }: ${ value }`);
}
// 0: 0
// 1: 10
// 2: 20
```

It should be clear that there's only one `value` declared per scope instance. But what about `i`? Is it being "re-declared"?

To answer that, consider what scope `i` is in. It might seem like it would be in the outer (in this case, global) scope, but it's not. It's in the scope of `for`-loop body, just like `value` is. In fact, you could sorta think about that loop in this more verbose equivalent form:

```
{
    // a fictional variable for illustration
    let $$i = 0;

    for ( /* nothing */; $$i < 3; $$i++) {
        // here's our actual loop `i`!
        let i = $$i;

        let value = i * 10;
        console.log(`${ i }: ${ value }`);
    }
    // 0: 0
    // 1: 10
    // 2: 20
}
```

Now it should be clear: the `i` and `value` variables are both declared exactly once **per scope instance**. No "re-declaration" here.

What about other `for`-loop forms?

```
for (let index in students) {
    // this is fine
}

for (let student of students) {
    // so is this
}
```

Same thing with `for..in` and `for..of` loops: the declared variable is treated as *inside* the loop body, and thus is handled per iteration (aka, per scope instance). No "re-declaration."

OK, I know you're thinking that I sound like a broken record at this point. But let's explore how `const` impacts these looping constructs. Consider:

```
var keepGoing = true;
while (keepGoing) {
    // ooo, a shiny constant!
    const value = Math.random();
    if (value > 0.5) {
        keepGoing = false;
    }
}
```

Just like the `let` variant of this program we saw earlier, `const` is being run exactly once within each loop iteration, so it's safe from "re-declaration" troubles. But things get more complicated when we talk about `for`-loops.

`for..in` and `for..of` are fine to use with `const`:

```
for (const index in students) {
    // this is fine
}

for (const student of students) {
    // this is also fine
}
```

But not the general `for`-loop:

```
for (const i = 0; i < 3; i++) {
    // oops, this is going to fail with
    // a Type Error after the first iteration
}
```

What's wrong here? We could use `let` just fine in this construct, and we asserted that it creates a new `i` for each loop iteration scope, so it doesn't even seem to be a "re-declaration."

Let's mentally "expand" that loop like we did earlier:

```
{
    // a fictional variable for illustration
    const $$i = 0;

    for ( ; $$i < 3; $$i++) {
        // here's our actual loop `i`!
        const i = $$i;
        // ..
    }
}
```

Do you spot the problem? Our `i` is indeed just created once inside the loop. That's not the problem. The problem is the conceptual `$$i` that must be incremented each time with the `$$i++` expression. That's **re-assignment** (not "re-declaration"), which isn't allowed for constants.

Remember, this "expanded" form is only a conceptual model to help you intuit the source of the problem. You might wonder if JS could have effectively made the `const $$i = 0` instead into `let $ii = 0`, which would then allow `const` to work with our classic `for`-loop? It's possible, but then it could have introduced potentially surprising exceptions to `for`-loop semantics.

For example, it would have been a rather arbitrary (and likely confusing) nuanced exception to allow `i++` in the `for`-loop header to skirt strictness of the `const` assignment, but not allow other re-assignments of `i` inside the loop iteration, as is sometimes useful.

The straightforward answer is: `const` can't be used with the classic `for`-loop form because of the required re-assignment.

Interestingly, if you don't do re-assignment, then it's valid:

```
var keepGoing = true;

for (const i = 0; keepGoing; /* nothing here */ ) {
    keepGoing = (Math.random() > 0.5);
    // ..
}
```

That works, but it's pointless. There's no reason to declare `i` in that position with a `const`, since the whole point of such a variable in that position is **to be used for counting iterations**. Just use a different loop form, like a `while` loop, or use a `let`!

Uninitialized Variables (aka, TDZ)

With `var` declarations, the variable is "hoisted" to the top of its scope. But it's also automatically initialized to the `undefined` value, so that the variable can be used throughout the entire scope.

However, `let` and `const` declarations are not quite the same in this respect.

Consider:

```
console.log(studentName);
// ReferenceError

let studentName = "Suzy";
```

The result of this program is that a `ReferenceError` is thrown on the first line. Depending on your JS environment, the error message may say something like: "Cannot access studentName before initialization."

Note

The error message as seen here used to be much more vague or misleading. Thankfully, several of us in the community were successfully able to lobby for JS engines to improve this error message so it more accurately tells you what's wrong!

That error message is quite indicative of what's wrong: `studentName` exists on line 1, but it's not been initialized, so it cannot be used yet. Let's try this:

```
studentName = "Suzy";   // let's try to initialize it!
// ReferenceError

console.log(studentName);

let studentName;
```

Oops. We still get the `ReferenceError`, but now on the first line where we're trying to assign to (aka, initialize!) this so-called "uninitialized" variable `studentName`. What's the deal!?

The real question is, how do we initialize an uninitialized variable? For `let`/`const`, the **only way** to do so is with an assignment attached to a declaration statement. An assignment by itself is insufficient! Consider:

```
let studentName = "Suzy";
console.log(studentName);   // Suzy
```

Here, we are initializing the `studentName` (in this case, to `"Suzy"` instead of `undefined`) by way of the `let` declaration statement form that's coupled with an assignment.

Alternatively:

```
// ..

let studentName;
// or:
// let studentName = undefined;

// ..

studentName = "Suzy";

console.log(studentName);
// Suzy
```

> **Note**
>
> That's interesting! Recall from earlier, we said that `var studentName;` is *not* the same as `var studentName = undefined;`, but here with `let`, they behave the same. The difference comes down to the fact that `var studentName` automatically initializes at the top of the scope, where `let studentName` does not.

Remember that we've asserted a few times so far that *Compiler* ends up removing any `var`/`let`/`const` declarators, replacing them with the instructions at the top of each scope to register the appropriate identifiers.

So if we analyze what's going on here, we see that an additional nuance is that *Compiler* is also adding an instruction in the middle of the program, at the point where the variable `studentName` was declared, to handle that declaration's auto-initialization. We cannot use the variable at any point prior to that initialization occuring. The same goes for `const` as it does for `let`.

The term coined by TC39 to refer to this *period of time* from the entering of a scope to where the auto-initialization of the variable occurs is: Temporal Dead Zone (TDZ).

The TDZ is the time window where a variable exists but is still uninitialized, and therefore cannot be accessed in any way. Only the execution of the instructions left by *Compiler* at the point of the original declaration can do that initialization. After that moment, the TDZ is done, and the variable is free to be used for the rest of the scope.

A `var` also has technically has a TDZ, but it's zero in length and thus unobservable to our programs! Only `let` and `const` have an observable TDZ.

By the way, "temporal" in TDZ does indeed refer to *time* not *position in code*. Consider:

```
askQuestion();
// ReferenceError

let studentName = "Suzy";

function askQuestion() {
    console.log(`${ studentName }, do you know?`);
}
```

Even though positionally the `console.log(..)` referencing `studentName` comes *after* the `let studentName` declaration, timing wise the `askQuestion()` function is invoked *before* the `let` statement is encountered, while `studentName` is still in its TDZ! Hence the error.

There's a common misconception that TDZ means `let` and `const` do not hoist. This is an inaccurate, or at least slightly misleading, claim. They definitely hoist.

The actual difference is that `let`/`const` declarations do not automatically initialize at the beginning of the scope, the way `var` does. The *debate* then is if the auto-initialization is *part of* hoisting, or not? I think auto-registration of a variable at the top of the scope (i.e., what I call "hoisting") and auto-initialization at the top of the scope (to `undefined`) are distinct operations and shouldn't be lumped together under the single term "hoisting."

We've already seen that `let` and `const` don't auto-initialize at the top of the scope. But let's prove that `let` and `const` *do* hoist (auto-register at the top of the scope), courtesy of our friend shadowing (see "Shadowing" in Chapter 3):

```
var studentName = "Kyle";

{
    console.log(studentName);
    // ???

    // ..

    let studentName = "Suzy";

    console.log(studentName);
    // Suzy
}
```

What's going to happen with the first `console.log(..)` statement? If `let studentName` didn't hoist to the top of the scope, then the first `console.log(..)` *should* print `"Kyle"`, right? At that moment, it would seem, only the outer `studentName` exists, so that's the variable `console.log(..)` should access and print.

But instead, the first `console.log(..)` throws a TDZ error, because in fact, the inner scope's `studentName` **was** hoisted (auto-registered at the top of the scope). What **didn't** happen (yet!) was the auto-initialization of that inner `studentName`; it's still uninitialized at that moment, hence the TDZ violation!

So to summarize, TDZ errors occur because `let`/`const` declarations *do* hoist their declarations to the top of their scopes, but unlike `var`, they defer the auto-initialization of their variables until the moment in the code's sequencing where the original declaration appeared. This window of time (hint: temporal), whatever its length, is the TDZ.

How can you avoid TDZ errors?

My advice: always put your `let` and `const` declarations at the top of any scope. Shrink the TDZ window to zero (or near zero) length, and then it'll be moot.

But why is TDZ even a thing? Why didn't TC39 dictate that `let`/`const` auto-initialize the way `var` does? Just be patient, we'll come back to explore the *why* of TDZ in Appendix A.

Finally Initialized

Working with variables has much more nuance than it seems at first glance. *Hoisting*, *(re)declaration*, and the *TDZ* are common sources of confusion for developers, especially those who have worked in other languages before coming to JS.

Before moving on, make sure your mental model is fully grounded on these aspects of JS scope and variables.

Hoisting is generally cited as an explicit mechanism of the JS engine, but it's really more a metaphor to describe the various ways JS handles variable declarations during compilation. But even as a metaphor, hoisting offers useful structure for thinking about the life-cycle of a variable—when it's created, when it's available to use, when it goes away.

Declaration and re-declaration of variables tend to cause confusion when thought of as runtime operations. But if you shift to compile-time thinking for these operations, the quirks and *shadows* diminish.

The TDZ (temporal dead zone) error is strange and frustrating when encountered. Fortunately, TDZ is relatively straightforward to avoid if you're always careful to place `let`/`const` declarations at the top of any scope.

As you successfully navigate these twists and turns of variable scope, the next chapter will lay out the factors that guide our decisions to place our declarations in various scopes, especially nested blocks.

Chapter 6: Limiting Scope Exposure

So far our focus has been explaining the mechanics of how scopes and variables work. With that foundation now firmly in place, our attention raises to a higher level of thinking: decisions and patterns we apply across the whole program.

To begin, we're going to look at how and why we should be using different levels of scope (functions and blocks) to organize our program's variables, specifically to reduce scope over-exposure.

Least Exposure

It makes sense that functions define their own scopes. But why do we need blocks to create scopes as well?

Software engineering articulates a fundamental discipline, typically applied to software security, called "The Principle of Least Privilege" (POLP). [1] And a variation of this principle that applies to our current discussion is typically labeled as "Least Exposure" (POLE).

POLP expresses a defensive posture to software architecture: components of the system should be designed to function with least privilege, least access, least exposure. If each piece is

[1] *Principle of Least Privilege*, https://en.wikipedia.org/wiki/Principle_of_least_privilege, 3 March 2020.

connected with minimum-necessary capabilities, the overall system is stronger from a security standpoint, because a compromise or failure of one piece has a minimized impact on the rest of the system.

If POLP focuses on system-level component design, the POLE *Exposure* variant focuses on a lower level; we'll apply it to how scopes interact with each other.

In following POLE, what do we want to minimize the exposure of? Simply: the variables registered in each scope.

Think of it this way: why shouldn't you just place all the variables of your program out in the global scope? That probably immediately feels like a bad idea, but it's worth considering why that is. When variables used by one part of the program are exposed to another part of the program, via scope, there are three main hazards that often arise:

- **Naming Collisions**: if you use a common and useful variable/function name in two different parts of the program, but the identifier comes from one shared scope (like the global scope), then name collision occurs, and it's very likely that bugs will occur as one part uses the variable/function in a way the other part doesn't expect.

  For example, imagine if all your loops used a single global `i` index variable, and then it happens that one loop in a function is running during an iteration of a loop from another function, and now the shared `i` variable gets an unexpected value.
- **Unexpected Behavior**: if you expose variables/functions whose usage is otherwise *private* to a piece of the program, it allows other developers to use them in ways you didn't intend, which can violate expected behavior and cause bugs.

For example, if your part of the program assumes an array contains all numbers, but someone else's code accesses and modifies the array to include booleans and strings, your code may then misbehave in unexpected ways.

Worse, exposure of *private* details invites those with mal-intent to try to work around limitations you have imposed, to do things with your part of the software that shouldn't be allowed.

- **Unintended Dependency**: if you expose variables/functions unnecessarily, it invites other developers to use and depend on those otherwise *private* pieces. While that doesn't break your program today, it creates a refactoring hazard in the future, because now you cannot as easily refactor that variable or function without potentially breaking other parts of the software that you don't control.

  For example, if your code relies on an array of numbers, and you later decide it's better to use some other data structure instead of an array, you now must take on the liability of adjusting other affected parts of the software.

POLE, as applied to variable/function scoping, essentially says, default to exposing the bare minimum necessary, keeping everything else as private as possible. Declare variables in as small and deeply nested of scopes as possible, rather than placing everything in the global (or even outer function) scope.

If you design your software accordingly, you have a much greater chance of avoiding (or at least minimizing) these three hazards.

Consider:

```
function diff(x,y) {
    if (x > y) {
        let tmp = x;
        x = y;
        y = tmp;
    }

    return y - x;
}

diff(3,7);      // 4
diff(7,5);      // 2
```

In this `diff(..)` function, we want to ensure that `y` is greater than or equal to `x`, so that when we subtract (`y - x`), the result is `0` or larger. If `x` is initially larger (the result would be negative!), we swap `x` and `y` using a `tmp` variable, to keep the result positive.

In this simple example, it doesn't seem to matter whether `tmp` is inside the `if` block or whether it belongs at the function level—it certainly shouldn't be a global variable! However, following the POLE principle, `tmp` should be as hidden in scope as possible. So we block scope `tmp` (using `let`) to the `if` block.

Hiding in Plain (Function) Scope

It should now be clear why it's important to hide our variable and function declarations in the lowest (most deeply nested) scopes possible. But how do we do so?

We've already seen the `let` and `const` keywords, which are block scoped declarators; we'll come back to them in more detail shortly. But first, what about hiding `var` or `function` declarations in scopes? That can easily be done by wrapping a `function` scope around a declaration.

Let's consider an example where `function` scoping can be useful.

The mathematical operation "factorial" (notated as "6!") is the multiplication of a given integer against all successively lower integers down to `1`—actually, you can stop at `2` since multiplying `1` does nothing. In other words, "6!" is the same as "6 * 5!", which is the same as "6 * 5 * 4!", and so on. Because of the nature of the math involved, once any given integer's factorial (like "4!") has been calculated, we shouldn't need to do that work again, as it'll always be the same answer.

So if you naively calculate factorial for `6`, then later want to calculate factorial for `7`, you might unnecessarily re-calculate the factorials of all the integers from 2 up to 6. If you're willing to trade memory for speed, you can solve that wasted computation by caching each integer's factorial as it's calculated:

```
var cache = {};

function factorial(x) {
    if (x < 2) return 1;
    if (!(x in cache)) {
        cache[x] = x * factorial(x - 1);
    }
    return cache[x];
}

factorial(6);
// 720

cache;
```

```
// {
//     "2": 2,
//     "3": 6,
//     "4": 24,
//     "5": 120,
//     "6": 720
// }

factorial(7);
// 5040
```

We're storing all the computed factorials in `cache` so that across multiple calls to `factorial(..)`, the previous computations remain. But the `cache` variable is pretty obviously a *private* detail of how `factorial(..)` works, not something that should be exposed in an outer scope—especially not the global scope.

> **Note**
>
> `factorial(..)` here is recursive—a call to itself is made from inside—but that's just for brevity of code sake; a non-recursive implementation would yield the same scoping analysis with respect to `cache`.

However, fixing this over-exposure issue is not as simple as hiding the `cache` variable inside `factorial(..)`, as it might seem. Since we need `cache` to survive multiple calls, it must be located in a scope outside that function. So what can we do?

Define another middle scope (between the outer/global scope and the inside of `factorial(..)`) for `cache` to be located:

```
// outer/global scope

function hideTheCache() {
    // "middle scope", where we hide `cache`
    var cache = {};

    return factorial;

    // **********************

    function factorial(x) {
        // inner scope
        if (x < 2) return 1;
        if (!(x in cache)) {
            cache[x] = x * factorial(x - 1);
        }
        return cache[x];
    }
}

var factorial = hideTheCache();

factorial(6);
// 720

factorial(7);
// 5040
```

The `hideTheCache()` function serves no other purpose than to create a scope for `cache` to persist in across multiple calls to `factorial(..)`. But for `factorial(..)` to have access to `cache`, we have to define `factorial(..)` inside that same scope. Then we return the function reference, as a value from `hideTheCache()`, and store it in an outer scope variable, also named `factorial`. Now as we call `factorial(..)` (multiple times!), its persistent `cache` stays hidden yet accessible only to `factorial(..)`!

OK, but... it's going to be tedious to define (and name!) a `hideTheCache(..)` function scope each time such a need for variable/function hiding occurs, especially since we'll likely want to avoid name collisions with this function by giving each occurrence a unique name. Ugh.

Note

The illustrated technique—caching a function's computed output to optimize performance when repeated calls of the same inputs are expected—is quite common in the Functional Programming (FP) world, canonically referred to as "memoization"; this caching relies on closure (see Chapter 7). Also, there are memory usage concerns (addressed in "A Word About Memory" in Appendix B). FP libraries will usually provide an optimized and vetted utility for memoization of functions, which would take the place of `hideTheCache(..)` here. Memoization is beyond the *scope* (pun intended!) of our discussion, but see my *Functional-Light JavaScript* book for more information.

Rather than defining a new and uniquely named function each time one of those scope-only-for-the-purpose-of-hiding-a-variable situations occurs, a perhaps better solution is to use a function expression:

```
var factorial = (function hideTheCache() {
    var cache = {};

    function factorial(x) {
        if (x < 2) return 1;
        if (!(x in cache)) {
            cache[x] = x * factorial(x - 1);
        }
        return cache[x];
    }

    return factorial;
})();

factorial(6);
// 720

factorial(7);
// 5040
```

Wait! This is still using a function to create the scope for hiding `cache`, and in this case, the function is still named `hideTheCache`, so how does that solve anything?

Recall from "Function Name Scope" (in Chapter 3), what happens to the name identifier from a `function` expression. Since `hideTheCache(..)` is defined as a `function` expression instead of a `function` declaration, its name is in its own scope—essentially the same scope as `cache`—rather than in the outer/global scope.

That means we can name every single occurrence of such a function expression the exact same name, and never have any collision. More appropriately, we can name each occurrence semantically based on whatever it is we're trying to hide, and not worry that whatever name we choose is going to collide with any other `function` expression scope in the program.

In fact, we *could* just leave off the name entirely—thus defining an "anonymous `function` expression" instead. But Appendix A will discuss the importance of names even for such scope-only functions.

Invoking Function Expressions Immediately

There's another important bit in the previous factorial recursive program that's easy to miss: the line at the end of the `function` expression that contains `})();`.

Notice that we surrounded the entire `function` expression in a set of `( .. )`, and then on the end, we added that second `()` parentheses set; that's actually calling the `function` expression we just defined. Moreover, in this case, the first set of surrounding `( .. )` around the function expression is not strictly necessary (more on that in a moment), but we used them for readability sake anyway.

So, in other words, we're defining a `function` expression that's then immediately invoked. This common pattern has a (very creative!) name: Immediately Invoked Function Expression (IIFE).

An IIFE is useful when we want to create a scope to hide variables/functions. Since it's an expression, it can be used in **any** place in a JS program where an expression is allowed. An IIFE can be named, as with `hideTheCache()`, or (much more commonly!) unnamed/anonymous. And it can be standalone or, as before, part of another statement—`hideTheCache()` returns the `factorial()` function reference which is then `=` assigned to the variable `factorial`.

For comparison, here's an example of a standalone IIFE:

```
// outer scope

(function(){
    // inner hidden scope
})();

// more outer scope
```

Unlike earlier with `hideTheCache()`, where the outer surrounding `(..)` were noted as being an optional stylistic choice, for a standalone IIFE they're **required**; they distinguish the `function` as an expression, not a statement. For consistency, however, always surround an IIFE `function` with `( .. )`.

> **Note**
>
> Technically, the surrounding `( .. )` aren't the only syntactic way to ensure the `function` in an IIFE is treated by the JS parser as a function expression. We'll look at some other options in Appendix A.

Function Boundaries

Beware that using an IIFE to define a scope can have some unintended consequences, depending on the code around it. Because an IIFE is a full function, the function boundary alters the behavior of certain statements/constructs.

For example, a `return` statement in some piece of code would change its meaning if an IIFE is wrapped around it, because now the `return` would refer to the IIFE's function. Non-arrow function IIFEs also change the binding of a `this` keyword—more on that in the *Objects & Classes* book. And statements like `break` and `continue` won't operate across an IIFE function boundary to control an outer loop or block.

So, if the code you need to wrap a scope around has `return`, `this`, `break`, or `continue` in it, an IIFE is probably not the best approach. In that case, you might look to create the scope with a block instead of a function.

Scoping with Blocks

You should by this point feel fairly comfortable with the merits of creating scopes to limit identifier exposure.

So far, we looked at doing this via `function` (i.e., IIFE) scope. But let's now consider using `let` declarations with nested blocks. In general, any `{ .. }` curly-brace pair which is a statement will act as a block, but **not necessarily** as a scope.

A block only becomes a scope if necessary, to contain its block-scoped declarations (i.e., `let` or `const`). Consider:

```
{
    // not necessarily a scope (yet)

    // ..

    // now we know the block needs to be a scope
    let thisIsNowAScope = true;

    for (let i = 0; i < 5; i++) {
        // this is also a scope, activated each
        // iteration
```

```
        if (i % 2 == 0) {
            // this is just a block, not a scope
            console.log(i);
        }
    }
}
// 0 2 4
```

Not all `{ .. }` curly-brace pairs create blocks (and thus are eligible to become scopes):

- Object literals use `{ .. }` curly-brace pairs to delimit their key-value lists, but such object values are **not** scopes.
- `class` uses `{ .. }` curly-braces around its body definition, but this is not a block or scope.
- A `function` uses `{ .. }` around its body, but this is not technically a block—it's a single statement for the function body. It *is*, however, a (function) scope.
- The `{ .. }` curly-brace pair on a `switch` statement (around the set of `case` clauses) does not define a block/scope.

Other than such non-block examples, a `{ .. }` curly-brace pair can define a block attached to a statement (like an `if` or `for`), or stand alone by itself—see the outermost `{ .. }` curly brace pair in the previous snippet. An explicit block of this sort—if it has no declarations, it's not actually a scope—serves no operational purpose, though it can still be useful as a semantic signal.

Explicit standalone `{ .. }` blocks have always been valid JS syntax, but since they couldn't be a scope prior to ES6's `let/const`, they are quite rare. However, post ES6, they're starting to catch on a little bit.

In most languages that support block scoping, an explicit block scope is an extremely common pattern for creating a narrow slice of scope for one or a few variables. So following the POLE principle, we should embrace this pattern more widespread in JS as well; use (explicit) block scoping to narrow the exposure of identifiers to the minimum practical.

An explicit block scope can be useful even inside of another block (whether the outer block is a scope or not).

For example:

```
if (somethingHappened) {
    // this is a block, but not a scope

    {
        // this is both a block and an
        // explicit scope
        let msg = somethingHappened.message();
        notifyOthers(msg);
    }

    // ..

    recoverFromSomething();
}
```

Here, the `{ .. }` curly-brace pair **inside** the `if` statement is an even smaller inner explicit block scope for `msg`, since that variable is not needed for the entire `if` block. Most developers would just block-scope `msg` to the `if` block and move on. And to be fair, when there's only a few lines to consider, it's a toss-up judgement call. But as code grows, these over-exposure issues become more pronounced.

So does it matter enough to add the extra `{ .. }` pair and indentation level? I think you should follow POLE and always (within reason!) define the smallest block for each variable. So I recommend using the extra explicit block scope as shown.

Recall the discussion of TDZ errors from "Uninitialized Variables (TDZ)" (Chapter 5). My suggestion there was: to minimize the risk of TDZ errors with `let`/`const` declarations, always put those declarations at the top of their scope.

If you find yourself placing a `let` declaration in the middle of a scope, first think, "Oh, no! TDZ alert!" If this `let` declaration isn't needed in the first half of that block, you should use an inner explicit block scope to further narrow its exposure!

Another example with an explicit block scope:

```
function getNextMonthStart(dateStr) {
    var nextMonth, year;

    {
        let curMonth;
        [ , year, curMonth ] = dateStr.match(
                /(\d{4})-(\d{2})-\d{2}/
            ) || [];
        nextMonth = (Number(curMonth) % 12) + 1;
    }

    if (nextMonth == 1) {
        year++;
    }

    return `${ year }-${
            String(nextMonth).padStart(2,"0")
        }-01`;
}
getNextMonthStart("2019-12-25");    // 2020-01-01
```

Let's first identify the scopes and their identifiers:

1. The outer/global scope has one identifier, the function `getNextMonthStart(..)`.
2. The function scope for `getNextMonthStart(..)` has three: `dateStr` (parameter), `nextMonth`, and `year`.
3. The `{ .. }` curly-brace pair defines an inner block scope that includes one variable: `curMonth`.

So why put `curMonth` in an explicit block scope instead of just alongside `nextMonth` and `year` in the top-level function scope? Because `curMonth` is only needed for those first two statements; at the function scope level it's over-exposed.

This example is small, so the hazards of over-exposing `curMonth` are pretty limited. But the benefits of the POLE principle are best achieved when you adopt the mindset of minimizing scope exposure by default, as a habit. If you follow the principle consistently even in the small cases, it will serve you more as your programs grow.

Let's now look at an even more substantial example:

```
function sortNamesByLength(names) {
    var buckets = [];

    for (let firstName of names) {
        if (buckets[firstName.length] == null) {
            buckets[firstName.length] = [];
        }
        buckets[firstName.length].push(firstName);
    }

    // a block to narrow the scope
    {
```

```
        let sortedNames = [];

        for (let bucket of buckets) {
            if (bucket) {
                // sort each bucket alphanumerically
                bucket.sort();

                // append the sorted names to our
                // running list
                sortedNames = [
                    ...sortedNames,
                    ...bucket
                ];
            }
        }

        return sortedNames;
    }
}

sortNamesByLength([
    "Sally",
    "Suzy",
    "Frank",
    "John",
    "Jennifer",
    "Scott"
]);
// [ "John", "Suzy", "Frank", "Sally",
//   "Scott", "Jennifer" ]
```

There are six identifiers declared across five different scopes. Could all of these variables have existed in the single outer/global scope? Technically, yes, since they're all uniquely named and thus have no name collisions. But this would be really poor code organization, and would likely lead to both confusion and future bugs.

We split them out into each inner nested scope as appropriate. Each variable is defined at the innermost scope possible for the program to operate as desired.

`sortedNames` could have been defined in the top-level function scope, but it's only needed for the second half of this function. To avoid over-exposing that variable in a higher level scope, we again follow POLE and block-scope it in the inner explicit block scope.

`var` *and* `let`

Next, let's talk about the declaration `var buckets`. That variable is used across the entire function (except the final `return` statement). Any variable that is needed across all (or even most) of a function should be declared so that such usage is obvious.

> **Note**
>
> The parameter `names` isn't used across the whole function, but there's no way limit the scope of a parameter, so it behaves as a function-wide declaration regardless.

So why did we use `var` instead of `let` to declare the `buckets` variable? There's both semantic and technical reasons to choose `var` here.

Stylistically, `var` has always, from the earliest days of JS, signaled "variable that belongs to a whole function." As we asserted in "Lexical Scope" (Chapter 1), `var` attaches to the nearest enclosing function scope, no matter where it appears. That's true even if `var` appears inside a block:

```
function diff(x,y) {
    if (x > y) {
        var tmp = x;    // `tmp` is function-scoped
        x = y;
        y = tmp;
    }

    return y - x;
}
```

Even though `var` is inside a block, its declaration is function-scoped (to `diff(..)`), not block-scoped.

While you can declare `var` inside a block (and still have it be function-scoped), I would recommend against this approach except in a few specific cases (discussed in Appendix A). Otherwise, `var` should be reserved for use in the top-level scope of a function.

Why not just use `let` in that same location? Because `var` is visually distinct from `let` and therefore signals clearly, "this variable is function-scoped." Using `let` in the top-level scope, especially if not in the first few lines of a function, and when all the other declarations in blocks use `let`, does not visually draw attention to the difference with the function-scoped declaration.

In other words, I feel `var` better communicates function-scoped than `let` does, and `let` both communicates (and achieves!) block-scoping where `var` is insufficient. As long as your programs are going to need both function-scoped and block-scoped variables, the most sensible and readable approach is to use both `var` *and* `let` together, each for their own best purpose.

There are other semantic and operational reasons to choose `var` or `let` in different scenarios. We'll explore the case for `var` *and* `let` in more detail in Appendix A.

> **Warning**
>
> My recommendation to use both `var` *and* `let` is clearly controversial and contradicts the majority. It's far more common to hear assertions like, "var is broken, let fixes it" and, "never use var, let is the replacement." Those opinions are valid, but they're merely opinions, just like mine. `var` is not factually broken or deprecated; it has worked since early JS and it will continue to work as long as JS is around.

Where To `let`?

My advice to reserve `var` for (mostly) only a top-level function scope means that most other declarations should use `let`. But you may still be wondering how to decide where each declaration in your program belongs?

POLE already guides you on those decisions, but let's make sure we explicitly state it. The way to decide is not based on which keyword you want to use. The way to decide is to ask, "What is the most minimal scope exposure that's sufficient for this variable?"

Once that is answered, you'll know if a variable belongs in a block scope or the function scope. If you decide initially that a variable should be block-scoped, and later realize it needs to be elevated to be function-scoped, then that dictates a change not only in the location of that variable's declaration, but also the declarator keyword used. The decision-making process really should proceed like that.

If a declaration belongs in a block scope, use `let`. If it belongs in the function scope, use `var` (again, just my opinion).

But another way to sort of visualize this decision making is to consider the pre-ES6 version of a program. For example, let's recall `diff(..)` from earlier:

```
function diff(x,y) {
    var tmp;

    if (x > y) {
        tmp = x;
        x = y;
        y = tmp;
    }

    return y - x;
}
```

In this version of `diff(..)`, `tmp` is clearly declared in the function scope. Is that appropriate for `tmp`? I would argue, no. `tmp` is only needed for those few statements. It's not needed for the `return` statement. It should therefore be block-scoped.

Prior to ES6, we didn't have `let` so we couldn't *actually* block-scope it. But we could do the next-best thing in signaling our intent:

```
function diff(x,y) {
    if (x > y) {
        // `tmp` is still function-scoped, but
        // the placement here semantically
        // signals block-scoping
        var tmp = x;
        x = y;
        y = tmp;
    }

    return y - x;
}
```

Placing the `var` declaration for `tmp` inside the `if` statement signals to the reader of the code that `tmp` belongs to that block. Even though JS doesn't enforce that scoping, the semantic signal still has benefit for the reader of your code.

Following this perspective, you can find any `var` that's inside a block of this sort and switch it to `let` to enforce the semantic signal already being sent. That's proper usage of `let` in my opinion.

Another example that was historically based on `var` but which should now pretty much always use `let` is the `for` loop:

```
for (var i = 0; i < 5; i++) {
    // do something
}
```

No matter where such a loop is defined, the `i` should basically always be used only inside the loop, in which case POLE dictates it should be declared with `let` instead of `var`:

```
for (let i = 0; i < 5; i++) {
    // do something
}
```

Almost the only case where switching a var to a `let` in this way would "break" your code is if you were relying on accessing the loop's iterator (`i`) outside/after the loop, such as:

```
for (var i = 0; i < 5; i++) {
    if (checkValue(i)) {
        break;
    }
}

if (i < 5) {
    console.log("The loop stopped early!");
}
```

This usage pattern is not terribly uncommon, but most feel it smells like poor code structure. A preferable approach is to use another outer-scoped variable for that purpose:

```
var lastI;

for (let i = 0; i < 5; i++) {
    lastI = i;
    if (checkValue(i)) {
        break;
    }
}

if (lastI < 5) {
    console.log("The loop stopped early!");
}
```

`lastI` is needed across this whole scope, so it's declared with `var`. `i` is only needed in (each) loop iteration, so it's declared with `let`.

What's the Catch?

So far we've asserted that `var` and parameters are function-scoped, and `let`/`const` signal block-scoped declarations. There's one little exception to call out: the `catch` clause.

Since the introduction of `try..catch` back in ES3 (in 1999), the `catch` clause has used an additional (little-known) block-scoping declaration capability:

```
try {
    doesntExist();
}
catch (err) {
    console.log(err);
    // ReferenceError: 'doesntExist' is not defined
    // ^^^^ message printed from the caught exception

    let onlyHere = true;
    var outerVariable = true;
}

console.log(outerVariable);     // true

console.log(err);
// ReferenceError: 'err' is not defined
// ^^^^ this is another thrown (uncaught) exception
```

The `err` variable declared by the `catch` clause is block-scoped to that block. This `catch` clause block can hold other block-scoped declarations via `let`. But a `var` declaration inside this block still attaches to the outer function/global scope.

ES2019 (recently, at the time of writing) changed `catch` clauses so their declaration is optional; if the declaration is omitted, the `catch` block is no longer (by default) a scope; it's still a block, though!

So if you need to react to the condition *that an exception occurred* (so you can gracefully recover), but you don't care about the error value itself, you can omit the `catch` declaration:

```
try {
    doOptionOne();
}
catch {   // catch-declaration omitted
    doOptionTwoInstead();
}
```

This is a small but delightful simplification of syntax for a fairly common use case, and may also be slightly more performant in removing an unnecessary scope!

Function Declarations in Blocks (FiB)

We've seen now that declarations using `let` or `const` are block-scoped, and `var` declarations are function-scoped. So what about `function` declarations that appear directly inside blocks? As a feature, this is called "FiB."

We typically think of `function` declarations like they're the equivalent of a `var` declaration. So are they function-scoped like `var` is?

No and yes. I know... that's confusing. Let's dig in:

```
if (false) {
    function ask() {
        console.log("Does this run?");
    }
}
ask();
```

What do you expect for this program to do? Three reasonable outcomes:

1. The `ask()` call might fail with a `ReferenceError` exception, because the `ask` identifier is block-scoped to the `if` block scope and thus isn't available in the outer/-global scope.
2. The `ask()` call might fail with a `TypeError` exception, because the `ask` identifier exists, but it's `undefined` (since the `if` statement doesn't run) and thus not a callable function.
3. The `ask()` call might run correctly, printing out the "Does it run?" message.

Here's the confusing part: depending on which JS environment you try that code snippet in, you may get different results! This is one of those few crazy areas where existing legacy behavior betrays a predictable outcome.

The JS specification says that `function` declarations inside of blocks are block-scoped, so the answer should be (1). However, most browser-based JS engines (including v8, which comes from Chrome but is also used in Node) will behave as (2), meaning the identifier is scoped outside the `if` block but the function value is not automatically initialized, so it remains `undefined`.

Why are browser JS engines allowed to behave contrary to the specification? Because these engines already had certain behaviors around FiB before ES6 introduced block scoping, and there was concern that changing to adhere to the specification might break some existing website JS code. As such, an exception was made in Appendix B of the JS specification, which allows certain deviations for browser JS engines (only!).

Note

You wouldn't typically categorize Node as a browser JS environment, since it usually runs on a server. But Node's v8 engine is shared with Chrome (and Edge) browsers. Since v8 is first a browser JS engine, it adopts this Appendix B exception, which then means that the browser exceptions are extended to Node.

One of the most common use cases for placing a `function` declaration in a block is to conditionally define a function one way or another (like with an `if..else` statement) depending on some environment state. For example:

```
if (typeof Array.isArray != "undefined") {
    function isArray(a) {
        return Array.isArray(a);
    }
}
else {
    function isArray(a) {
        return Object.prototype.toString.call(a)
            == "[object Array]";
    }
}
```

It's tempting to structure code this way for performance reasons, since the `typeof Array.isArray` check is only performed once, as opposed to defining just one `isArray(..)` and putting the `if` statement inside it—the check would then run unnecessarily on every call.

> **Warning**
>
> In addition to the risks of FiB deviations, another problem with conditional-definition of functions is it's harder to debug such a program. If you end up with a bug in the `isArray(..)` function, you first have to figure out *which* `isArray(..)` implementation is actually running! Sometimes, the bug is that the wrong one was applied because the conditional check was incorrect! If you define multiple versions of a function, that program is always harder to reason about and maintain.

In addition to the previous snippets, several other FiB corner cases are lurking; such behaviors in various browsers and non-browser JS environments (JS engines that aren't browser based) will likely vary. For example:

```
if (true) {
    function ask() {
        console.log("Am I called?");
    }
}

if (true) {
    function ask() {
        console.log("Or what about me?");
    }
```

```
}

for (let i = 0; i < 5; i++) {
    function ask() {
        console.log("Or is it one of these?");
    }
}

ask();

function ask() {
    console.log("Wait, maybe, it's this one?");
}
```

Recall that function hoisting as described in "When Can I Use a Variable?" (in Chapter 5) might suggest that the final `ask()` in this snippet, with "Wait, maybe..." as its message, would hoist above the call to `ask()`. Since it's the last function declaration of that name, it should "win," right? Unfortunately, no.

It's not my intention to document all these weird corner cases, nor to try to explain why each of them behaves a certain way. That information is, in my opinion, arcane legacy trivia.

My real concern with FiB is, what advice can I give to ensure your code behaves predictably in all circumstances?

As far as I'm concerned, the only practical answer to avoiding the vagaries of FiB is to simply avoid FiB entirely. In other words, never place a `function` declaration directly inside any block. Always place `function` declarations anywhere in the top-level scope of a function (or in the global scope).

So for the earlier `if..else` example, my suggestion is to avoid conditionally defining functions if at all possible. Yes, it may be slightly less performant, but this is the better overall approach:

```
function isArray(a) {
    if (typeof Array.isArray != "undefined") {
        return Array.isArray(a);
    }
    else {
        return Object.prototype.toString.call(a)
            == "[object Array]";
    }
}
```

If that performance hit becomes a critical path issue for your application, I suggest you consider this approach:

```
var isArray = function isArray(a) {
    return Array.isArray(a);
};

// override the definition, if you must
if (typeof Array.isArray == "undefined") {
    isArray = function isArray(a) {
        return Object.prototype.toString.call(a)
            == "[object Array]";
    };
}
```

It's important to notice that here I'm placing a `function` **expression**, not a declaration, inside the `if` statement. That's perfectly fine and valid, for `function` expressions to appear inside blocks. Our discussion about FiB is about avoiding `function` **declarations** in blocks.

Even if you test your program and it works correctly, the small benefit you may derive from using FiB style in your code is far outweighed by the potential risks in the future for confusion by other developers, or variances in how your code runs in other JS environments.

FiB is not worth it, and should be avoided.

Blocked Over

The point of lexical scoping rules in a programming language is so we can appropriately organize our program's variables, both for operational as well as semantic code communication purposes.

And one of the most important organizational techniques is to ensure that no variable is over-exposed to unnecessary scopes (POLE). Hopefully you now appreciate block scoping much more deeply than before.

Hopefully by you feel like you're standing on much more solid ground with understanding lexical scope. From that base, the next chapter jumps into the weighty topic of closure.

Chapter 7: Using Closures

Up to this point, we've focused on the ins and outs of lexical scope, and how that affects the organization and usage of variables in our programs.

Our attention again shifts broader in abstraction, to the historically somewhat daunting topic of closure. Don't worry! You don't need an advanced computer science degree to make sense of it. Our broad goal in this book is not merely to understand scope, but to more effectively use it in the structure of our programs; closure is central to that effort.

Recall the main conclusion of Chapter 6: the *least exposure* principle (POLE) encourages us to use block (and function) scoping to limit the scope exposure of variables. This helps keep code understandable and maintainable, and helps avoid many scoping pitfalls (i.e., name collision, etc.).

Closure builds on this approach: for variables we need to use over time, instead of placing them in larger outer scopes, we can encapsulate (more narrowly scope) them but still preserve access from inside functions, for broader use. Functions *remember* these referenced scoped variables via closure.

We already saw an example of this kind of closure in the previous chapter (`factorial(..)` in Chapter 6), and you've almost certainly already used it in your own programs. If you've ever written a callback that accesses variables outside its own scope... guess what!? That's closure.

Closure is one of the most important language characteristics ever invented in programming—it underlies major programming paradigms, including Functional Programming (FP), modules, and even a bit of class-oriented design. Getting comfortable with closure is required for mastering JS and effectively leveraging many important design patterns throughout your code.

Addressing all aspects of closure requires a daunting mountain of discussion and code throughout this chapter. Make sure to take your time and ensure you're comfortable with each bit before moving onto the next.

See the Closure

Closure is originally a mathematical concept, from lambda calculus. But I'm not going to list out math formulas or use a bunch of notation and jargon to define it.

Instead, I'm going to focus on a practical perspective. We'll start by defining closure in terms of what we can observe in different behavior of our programs, as opposed to if closure was not present in JS. However, later in this chapter, we're going to flip closure around to look at it from an *alternative perspective*.

Closure is a behavior of functions and only functions. If you aren't dealing with a function, closure does not apply. An object cannot have closure, nor does a class have closure (though its functions/methods might). Only functions have closure.

For closure to be observed, a function must be invoked, and specifically it must be invoked in a different branch of the scope chain from where it was originally defined. A function executing in the same scope it was defined would not exhibit any observably different behavior with or without closure being possible; by the observational perspective and definition, that is not closure.

Let's look at some code, annotated with its relevant scope bubble colors (see Chapter 2):

```
// outer/global scope: RED(1)

function lookupStudent(studentID) {
    // function scope: BLUE(2)

    var students = [
        { id: 14, name: "Kyle" },
        { id: 73, name: "Suzy" },
        { id: 112, name: "Frank" },
        { id: 6, name: "Sarah" }
    ];

    return function greetStudent(greeting){
        // function scope: GREEN(3)

        var student = students.find(
            student => student.id == studentID
        );

        return `${ greeting }, ${ student.name }!`;
    };
}

var chosenStudents = [
    lookupStudent(6),
    lookupStudent(112)
];
```

```
// accessing the function's name:
chosenStudents[0].name;
// greetStudent

chosenStudents[0]("Hello");
// Hello, Sarah!

chosenStudents[1]("Howdy");
// Howdy, Frank!
```

The first thing to notice about this code is that the `lookupStudent(..)` outer function creates and returns an inner function called `greetStudent(..)`. `lookupStudent(..)` is called twice, producing two separate instances of its inner `greetStudent(..)` function, both of which are saved into the `chosenStudents` array.

We verify that's the case by checking the `.name` property of the returned function saved in `chosenStudents[0]`, and it's indeed an instance of the inner `greetStudent(..)`.

After each call to `lookupStudent(..)` finishes, it would seem like all its inner variables would be discarded and GC'd (garbage collected). The inner function is the only thing that seems to be returned and preserved. But here's where the behavior differs in ways we can start to observe.

While `greetStudent(..)` does receive a single argument as the parameter named `greeting`, it also makes reference to both `students` and `studentID`, identifiers which come from the enclosing scope of `lookupStudent(..)`. Each of those references from the inner function to the variable in an outer scope is called a *closure*. In academic terms, each instance of `greetStudent(..)` *closes over* the outer variables `students` and `studentID`.

So what do those closures do here, in a concrete, observable sense?

Closure allows `greetStudent(..)` to continue to access those outer variables even after the outer scope is finished (when each call to `lookupStudent(..)` completes). Instead of the instances of `students` and `studentID` being GC'd, they stay around in memory. At a later time when either instance of the `greetStudent(..)` function is invoked, those variables are still there, holding their current values.

If JS functions did not have closure, the completion of each `lookupStudent(..)` call would immediately tear down its scope and GC the `students` and `studentID` variables. When we later called one of the `greetStudent(..)` functions, what would then happen?

If `greetStudent(..)` tried to access what it thought was a BLUE(2) marble, but that marble did not actually exist (anymore), the reasonable assumption is we should get a `ReferenceError`, right?

But we don't get an error. The fact that the execution of `chosenStudents[0]("Hello")` works and returns us the message "Hello, Sarah!", means it was still able to access the `students` and `studentID` variables. This is a direct observation of closure!

Pointed Closure

Actually, we glossed over a little detail in the previous discussion which I'm guessing many readers missed!

Because of how terse the syntax for `=>` arrow functions is, it's easy to forget that they still create a scope (as asserted in "Arrow Functions" in Chapter 3). The `student => student.id == studentID` arrow function is creating another scope bubble inside the `greetStudent(..)` function scope.

Building on the metaphor of colored buckets and bubbles from Chapter 2, if we were creating a colored diagram for this code, there's a fourth scope at this innermost nesting level, so we'd need a fourth color; perhaps we'd pick ORANGE(4) for that scope:

```
var student = students.find(
    student =>
        // function scope: ORANGE(4)
        student.id == studentID
);
```

The BLUE(2) `studentID` reference is actually inside the ORANGE(4) scope rather than the GREEN(3) scope of `greetStudent(..)`; also, the `student` parameter of the arrow function is ORANGE(4), shadowing the GREEN(3) `student`.

The consequence here is that this arrow function passed as a callback to the array's `find(..)` method has to hold the closure over `studentID`, rather than `greetStudent(..)` holding that closure. That's not too big of a deal, as everything still works as expected. It's just important not to skip over the fact that even tiny arrow functions can get in on the closure party.

Adding Up Closures

Let's examine one of the canonical examples often cited for closure:

```
function adder(num1) {
    return function addTo(num2){
        return num1 + num2;
    };
}

var add10To = adder(10);
var add42To = adder(42);

add10To(15);    // 25
add42To(9);     // 51
```

Each instance of the inner `addTo(..)` function is closing over its own `num1` variable (with values `10` and `42`, respectively), so those `num1`'s don't go away just because `adder(..)` finishes. When we later invoke one of those inner `addTo(..)` instances, such as the `add10To(15)` call, its closed-over `num1` variable still exists and still holds the original `10` value. The operation is thus able to perform `10 + 15` and return the answer `25`.

An important detail might have been too easy to gloss over in that previous paragraph, so let's reinforce it: closure is associated with an instance of a function, rather than its single lexical definition. In the preceding snippet, there's just one inner `addTo(..)` function defined inside `adder(..)`, so it might seem like that would imply a single closure.

But actually, every time the outer `adder(..)` function runs, a *new* inner `addTo(..)` function instance is created, and for each new instance, a new closure. So each inner function instance (labeled `add10To(..)` and `add42To(..)` in our program) has its own closure over its own instance of the scope environment from that execution of `adder(..)`.

Even though closure is based on lexical scope, which is

handled at compile time, closure is observed as a runtime characteristic of function instances.

Live Link, Not a Snapshot

In both examples from the previous sections, we **read the value from a variable** that was held in a closure. That makes it feel like closure might be a snapshot of a value at some given moment. Indeed, that's a common misconception.

Closure is actually a live link, preserving access to the full variable itself. We're not limited to merely reading a value; the closed-over variable can be updated (re-assigned) as well! By closing over a variable in a function, we can keep using that variable (read and write) as long as that function reference exists in the program, and from anywhere we want to invoke that function. This is why closure is such a powerful technique used widely across so many areas of programming!

Figure 4 depicts the function instances and scope links:

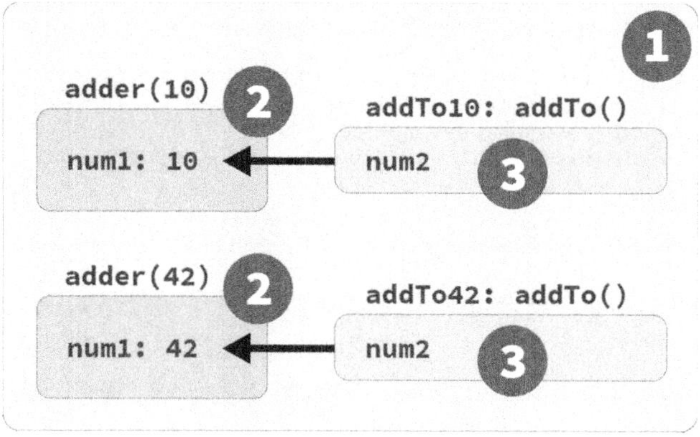

Fig. 4: Visualizing Closures

As shown in Figure 4, each call to `adder(..)` creates a new BLUE(2) scope containing a `num1` variable, as well as a new instance of `addTo(..)` function as a GREEN(3) scope. Notice that the function instances (`addTo10(..)` and `addTo42(..)`) are present in and invoked from the RED(1) scope.

Now let's examine an example where the closed-over variable is updated:

```
function makeCounter() {
    var count = 0;

    return function getCurrent(){
        count = count + 1;
        return count;
    };
}

var hits = makeCounter();

// later

hits();     // 1

// later

hits();     // 2
hits();     // 3
```

The `count` variable is closed over by the inner `getCurrent()` function, which keeps it around instead of it being subjected to GC. The `hits()` function calls access *and* update this variable, returning an incrementing count each time.

Though the enclosing scope of a closure is typically from a function, that's not actually required; there only needs to be an inner function present inside an outer scope:

```
var hits;
{   // an outer scope (but not a function)
    let count = 0;
    hits = function getCurrent(){
        count = count + 1;
        return count;
    };
}
hits();      // 1
hits();      // 2
hits();      // 3
```

> **Note**
>
> I deliberately defined `getCurrent()` as a `function` expression instead of a `function` declaration. This isn't about closure, but with the dangerous quirks of FiB (Chapter 6).

Because it's so common to mistake closure as value-oriented instead of variable-oriented, developers sometimes get tripped up trying to use closure to snapshot-preserve a value from some moment in time. Consider:

```
var studentName = "Frank";

var greeting = function hello() {
    // we are closing over `studentName`,
    // not "Frank"
    console.log(
        `Hello, ${ studentName }!`
    );
}
```

```
// later

studentName = "Suzy";

// later

greeting();
// Hello, Suzy!
```

By defining `greeting()` (aka, `hello()`) when `studentName` holds the value `"Frank"` (before the re-assignment to `"Suzy"`), the mistaken assumption is often that the closure will capture `"Frank"`. But `greeting()` is closed over the variable `studentName`, not its value. Whenever `greeting()` is invoked, the current value of the variable (`"Suzy"`, in this case) is reflected.

The classic illustration of this mistake is defining functions inside a loop:

```
var keeps = [];

for (var i = 0; i < 3; i++) {
    keeps[i] = function keepI(){
        // closure over `i`
        return i;
    };
}

keeps[0]();   // 3 -- WHY!?
keeps[1]();   // 3
keeps[2]();   // 3
```

> **Note**
>
> This kind of closure illustration typically uses a `setTimeout(..)` or some other callback like an event handler, inside the loop. I've simplified the example by storing function references in an array, so that we don't need to consider asynchronous timing in our analysis. The closure principle is the same, regardless.

You might have expected the `keeps[0]()` invocation to return `0`, since that function was created during the first iteration of the loop when `i` was `0`. But again, that assumption stems from thinking of closure as value-oriented rather than variable-oriented.

Something about the structure of a `for`-loop can trick us into thinking that each iteration gets its own new `i` variable; in fact, this program only has one `i` since it was declared with `var`.

Each saved function returns `3`, because by the end of the loop, the single `i` variable in the program has been assigned `3`. Each of the three functions in the `keeps` array do have individual closures, but they're all closed over that same shared `i` variable.

Of course, a single variable can only ever hold one value at any given moment. So if you want to preserve multiple values, you need a different variable for each.

How could we do that in the loop snippet? Let's create a new variable for each iteration:

```
var keeps = [];

for (var i = 0; i < 3; i++) {
    // new `j` created each iteration, which gets
    // a copy of the value of `i` at this moment
    let j = i;

    // the `i` here isn't being closed over, so
    // it's fine to immediately use its current
    // value in each loop iteration
    keeps[i] = function keepEachJ(){
        // close over `j`, not `i`!
        return j;
    };
}
keeps[0]();    // 0
keeps[1]();    // 1
keeps[2]();    // 2
```

Each function is now closed over a separate (new) variable from each iteration, even though all of them are named `j`. And each `j` gets a copy of the value of `i` at that point in the loop iteration; that `j` never gets re-assigned. So all three functions now return their expected values: `0`, `1`, and `2`!

Again remember, even if we were using asynchrony in this program, such as passing each inner `keepEachJ()` function into `setTimeout(..)` or some event handler subscription, the same kind of closure behavior would still be observed.

Recall the "Loops" section in Chapter 5, which illustrates how a `let` declaration in a `for` loop actually creates not just one variable for the loop, but actually creates a new variable for *each iteration* of the loop. That trick/quirk is exactly what we need for our loop closures:

```
var keeps = [];

for (let i = 0; i < 3; i++) {
    // the `let i` gives us a new `i` for
    // each iteration, automatically!
    keeps[i] = function keepEachI(){
        return i;
    };
}
keeps[0]();    // 0
keeps[1]();    // 1
keeps[2]();    // 2
```

Since we're using `let`, three `i`'s are created, one for each loop, so each of the three closures *just work* as expected.

Common Closures: Ajax and Events

Closure is most commonly encountered with callbacks:

```
function lookupStudentRecord(studentID) {
    ajax(
        `https://some.api/student/${ studentID }`,
        function onRecord(record) {
            console.log(
                `${ record.name } (${ studentID })`
            );
        }
    );
}

lookupStudentRecord(114);
// Frank (114)
```

The `onRecord(..)` callback is going to be invoked at some point in the future, after the response from the Ajax call comes back. This invocation will happen from the internals of the `ajax(..)` utility, wherever that comes from. Furthermore, when that happens, the `lookupStudentRecord(..)` call will long since have completed.

Why then is `studentID` still around and accessible to the callback? Closure.

Event handlers are another common usage of closure:

```
function listenForClicks(btn,label) {
    btn.addEventListener("click",function onClick(){
        console.log(
            `The ${ label } button was clicked!`
        );
    });
}

var submitBtn = document.getElementById("submit-btn");

listenForClicks(submitBtn,"Checkout");
```

The `label` parameter is closed over by the `onClick(..)` event handler callback. When the button is clicked, `label` still exists to be used. This is closure.

What If I Can't See It?

You've probably heard this common adage:

> If a tree falls in the forest but nobody is around to hear it, does it make a sound?

It's a silly bit of philosophical gymnastics. Of course from a scientific perspective, sound waves are created. But the real point: *does it matter* if the sound happens?

Remember, the emphasis in our definition of closure is observability. If a closure exists (in a technical, implementation, or academic sense) but it cannot be observed in our programs, *does it matter?* No.

To reinforce this point, let's look at some examples that are *not* observably based on closure.

For example, invoking a function that makes use of lexical scope lookup:

```
function say(myName) {
    var greeting = "Hello";
    output();

    function output() {
        console.log(
            `${ greeting }, ${ myName }!`
        );
    }
}

say("Kyle");
// Hello, Kyle!
```

The inner function `output()` accesses the variables `greeting` and `myName` from its enclosing scope. But the invocation of `output()` happens in that same scope, where of course `greeting` and `myName` are still available; that's just lexical scope, not closure.

Any lexically scoped language whose functions didn't support closure would still behave this same way.

In fact, global scope variables essentially cannot be (observably) closed over, because they're always accessible from everywhere. No function can ever be invoked in any part of the scope chain that is not a descendant of the global scope.

Consider:

```
var students = [
    { id: 14, name: "Kyle" },
    { id: 73, name: "Suzy" },
    { id: 112, name: "Frank" },
    { id: 6, name: "Sarah" }
];

function getFirstStudent() {
    return function firstStudent(){
        return students[0].name;
    };
}

var student = getFirstStudent();

student();
// Kyle
```

The inner `firstStudent()` function does reference `students`, which is a variable outside its own scope. But since `students` happens to be from the global scope, no matter where that function is invoked in the program, its ability to access `students` is nothing more special than normal lexical scope.

All function invocations can access global variables, regardless of whether closure is supported by the language or not. Global variables don't need to be closed over.

Variables that are merely present but never accessed don't result in closure:

```
function lookupStudent(studentID) {
    return function nobody(){
        var msg = "Nobody's here yet.";
        console.log(msg);
    };
}

var student = lookupStudent(112);

student();
// Nobody's here yet.
```

The inner function `nobody()` doesn't close over any outer variables—it only uses its own variable `msg`. Even though `studentID` is present in the enclosing scope, `studentID` is not referred to by `nobody()`. The JS engine doesn't need to keep `studentID` around after `lookupStudent(..)` has finished running, so GC wants to clean up that memory!

Whether JS functions support closure or not, this program would behave the same. Therefore, no observed closure here.

If there's no function invocation, closure can't be observed:

```
function greetStudent(studentName) {
    return function greeting(){
        console.log(
            `Hello, ${ studentName }!`
        );
    };
}

greetStudent("Kyle");

// nothing else happens
```

This one's tricky, because the outer function definitely does get invoked. But the inner function is the one that *could* have had closure, and yet it's never invoked; the returned function here is just thrown away. So even if technically the JS engine created closure for a brief moment, it was not observed in any meaningful way in this program.

A tree may have fallen... but we didn't hear it, so we don't care.

Observable Definition

We're now ready to define closure:

> Closure is observed when a function uses variable(s) from outer scope(s) even while running in a scope where those variable(s) wouldn't be accessible.

The key parts of this definition are:

- Must be a function involved
- Must reference at least one variable from an outer scope
- Must be invoked in a different branch of the scope chain from the variable(s)

This observation-oriented definition means we shouldn't dismiss closure as some indirect, academic trivia. Instead, we should look and plan for the direct, concrete effects closure has on our program behavior.

The Closure Lifecycle and Garbage Collection (GC)

Since closure is inherently tied to a function instance, its closure over a variable lasts as long as there is still a reference to that function.

If ten functions all close over the same variable, and over time nine of these function references are discarded, the lone remaining function reference still preserves that variable. Once that final function reference is discarded, the last closure over that variable is gone, and the variable itself is GC'd.

This has an important impact on building efficient and performant programs. Closure can unexpectedly prevent the GC of a variable that you're otherwise done with, which leads to run-away memory usage over time. That's why it's important to discard function references (and thus their closures) when they're not needed anymore.

Consider:

```
function manageBtnClickEvents(btn) {
    var clickHandlers = [];

    return function listener(cb){
        if (cb) {
            let clickHandler =
                function onClick(evt){
                    console.log("clicked!");
                    cb(evt);
                };
            clickHandlers.push(clickHandler);
            btn.addEventListener(
                "click",
```

```
                clickHandler
            );
        }
        else {
            // passing no callback unsubscribes
            // all click handlers
            for (let handler of clickHandlers) {
                btn.removeEventListener(
                    "click",
                    handler
                );
            }

            clickHandlers = [];
        }
    };
}

// var mySubmitBtn = ..
var onSubmit = manageBtnClickEvents(mySubmitBtn);

onSubmit(function checkout(evt){
    // handle checkout
});

onSubmit(function trackAction(evt){
    // log action to analytics
});

// later, unsubscribe all handlers:
onSubmit();
```

In this program, the inner `onClick(..)` function holds a closure over the passed in `cb` (the provided event callback). That means the `checkout()` and `trackAction()` function expression references are held via closure (and cannot be

GC'd) for as long as these event handlers are subscribed.

When we call `onSubmit()` with no input on the last line, all event handlers are unsubscribed, and the `clickHandlers` array is emptied. Once all click handler function references are discarded, the closures of `cb` references to `checkout()` and `trackAction()` are discarded.

When considering the overall health and efficiency of the program, unsubscribing an event handler when it's no longer needed can be even more important than the initial subscription!

Per Variable or Per Scope?

Another question we need to tackle: should we think of closure as applied only to the referenced outer variable(s), or does closure preserve the entire scope chain with all its variables?

In other words, in the previous event subscription snippet, is the inner `onClick(..)` function closed over only `cb`, or is it also closed over `clickHandler`, `clickHandlers`, and `btn`?

Conceptually, closure is **per variable** rather than *per scope*. Ajax callbacks, event handlers, and all other forms of function closures are typically assumed to close over only what they explicitly reference.

But the reality is more complicated than that.

Another program to consider:

```
function manageStudentGrades(studentRecords) {
    var grades = studentRecords.map(getGrade);

    return addGrade;

    // **********************

    function getGrade(record){
        return record.grade;
    }

    function sortAndTrimGradesList() {
        // sort by grades, descending
        grades.sort(function desc(g1,g2){
            return g2 - g1;
        });

        // only keep the top 10 grades
        grades = grades.slice(0,10);
    }

    function addGrade(newGrade) {
        grades.push(newGrade);
        sortAndTrimGradesList();
        return grades;
    }
}

var addNextGrade = manageStudentGrades([
    { id: 14, name: "Kyle", grade: 86 },
    { id: 73, name: "Suzy", grade: 87 },
    { id: 112, name: "Frank", grade: 75 },
    // ..many more records..
    { id: 6, name: "Sarah", grade: 91 }
]);
```

```
// later

addNextGrade(81);
addNextGrade(68);
// [ .., .., ... ]
```

The outer function `manageStudentGrades(..)` takes a list of student records, and returns an `addGrade(..)` function reference, which we externally label `addNextGrade(..)`. Each time we call `addNextGrade(..)` with a new grade, we get back a current list of the top 10 grades, sorted numerically descending (see `sortAndTrimGradesList()`).

From the end of the original `manageStudentGrades(..)` call, and between the multiple `addNextGrade(..)` calls, the `grades` variable is preserved inside `addGrade(..)` via closure; that's how the running list of top grades is maintained. Remember, it's a closure over the variable `grades` itself, not the array it holds.

That's not the only closure involved, however. Can you spot other variables being closed over?

Did you spot that `addGrade(..)` references `sortAndTrimGradesList`? That means it's also closed over that identifier, which happens to hold a reference to the `sortAndTrimGradesList()` function. That second inner function has to stay around so that `addGrade(..)` can keep calling it, which also means any variables *it* closes over stick around—though, in this case, nothing extra is closed over there.

What else is closed over?

Consider the `getGrade` variable (and its function); is it closed over? It's referenced in the outer scope of `manageStudentGrades(..)` in the `.map(getGrade)` call. But it's not referenced in `addGrade(..)` or `sortAndTrimGradesList()`.

What about the (potentially) large list of student records we pass in as `studentRecords`? Is that variable closed over? If it is, the array of student records is never getting GC'd, which leads to this program holding onto a larger amount of memory than we might assume. But if we look closely again, none of the inner functions reference `studentRecords`.

According to the *per variable* definition of closure, since `getGrade` and `studentRecords` are *not* referenced by the inner functions, they're not closed over. They should be freely available for GC right after the `manageStudentGrades(..)` call completes.

Indeed, try debugging this code in a recent JS engine, like v8 in Chrome, placing a breakpoint inside the `addGrade(..)` function. You may notice that the inspector **does not** list the `studentRecords` variable. That's proof, debugging-wise anyway, that the engine does not maintain `studentRecords` via closure. Phew!

But how reliable is this observation as proof? Consider this (rather contrived!) program:

```
function storeStudentInfo(id,name,grade) {
    return function getInfo(whichValue){
        // warning:
        //   using `eval(..)` is a bad idea!
        var val = eval(whichValue);
        return val;
    };
}

var info = storeStudentInfo(73,"Suzy",87);

info("name");
// Suzy
```

```
info("grade");
// 87
```

Notice that the inner function `getInfo(..)` is not explicitly closed over any of `id`, `name`, or `grade` variables. And yet, calls to `info(..)` seem to still be able to access the variables, albeit through use of the `eval(..)` lexical scope cheat (see Chapter 1).

So all the variables were definitely preserved via closure, despite not being explicitly referenced by the inner function. So does that disprove the *per variable* assertion in favor of *per scope*? Depends.

Many modern JS engines do apply an *optimization* that removes any variables from a closure scope that aren't explicitly referenced. However, as we see with `eval(..)`, there are situations where such an optimization cannot be applied, and the closure scope continues to contain all its original variables. In other words, closure must be *per scope*, implementation wise, and then an optional optimization trims down the scope to only what was closed over (a similar outcome as *per variable* closure).

Even as recent as a few years ago, many JS engines did not apply this optimization; it's possible your websites may still run in such browsers, especially on older or lower-end devices. That means it's possible that long-lived closures such as event handlers may be holding onto memory much longer than we would have assumed.

And the fact that it's an optional optimization in the first place, rather than a requirement of the specification, means that we shouldn't just casually over-assume its applicability.

In cases where a variable holds a large value (like an object or array) and that variable is present in a closure scope, if you don't need that value anymore and don't want that memory held, it's safer (memory usage) to manually discard the value rather than relying on closure optimization/GC.

Let's apply a *fix* to the earlier `manageStudentGrades(..)` example to ensure the potentially large array held in `studentRecords` is not caught up in a closure scope unnecessarily:

```
function manageStudentGrades(studentRecords) {
    var grades = studentRecords.map(getGrade);

    // unset `studentRecords` to prevent unwanted
    // memory retention in the closure
    studentRecords = null;

    return addGrade;
    // ..
}
```

We're not removing `studentRecords` from the closure scope; that we cannot control. We're ensuring that even if `studentRecords` remains in the closure scope, that variable is no longer referencing the potentially large array of data; the array can be GC'd.

Again, in many cases JS might automatically optimize the program to the same effect. But it's still a good habit to be careful and explicitly make sure we don't keep any significant amount of device memory tied up any longer than necessary.

As a matter of fact, we also technically don't need the function `getGrade()` anymore after the `.map(getGrade)` call completes. If profiling our application showed this was a critical area of excess memory use, we could possibly eek out a tiny bit more memory by freeing up that reference so its value isn't tied up either. That's likely unnecessary in this toy example, but this is a general technique to keep in mind if you're optimizing the memory footprint of your application.

The takeaway: it's important to know where closures appear in our programs, and what variables are included. We should manage these closures carefully so we're only holding onto what's minimally needed and not wasting memory.

An Alternative Perspective

Reviewing our working definition for closure, the assertion is that functions are "first-class values" that can be passed around the program, just like any other value. Closure is the link-association that connects that function to the scope/variables outside of itself, no matter where that function goes.

Let's recall a code example from earlier in this chapter, again with relevant scope bubble colors annotated:

```
// outer/global scope: RED(1)

function adder(num1) {
    // function scope: BLUE(2)

    return function addTo(num2){
        // function scope: GREEN(3)

        return num1 + num2;
    };
}
```

```
var add10To = adder(10);
var add42To = adder(42);

add10To(15);    // 25
add42To(9);     // 51
```

Our current perspective suggests that wherever a function is passed and invoked, closure preserves a hidden link back to the original scope to facilitate the access to the closed-over variables. Figure 4, repeated here for convenience, illustrates this notion:

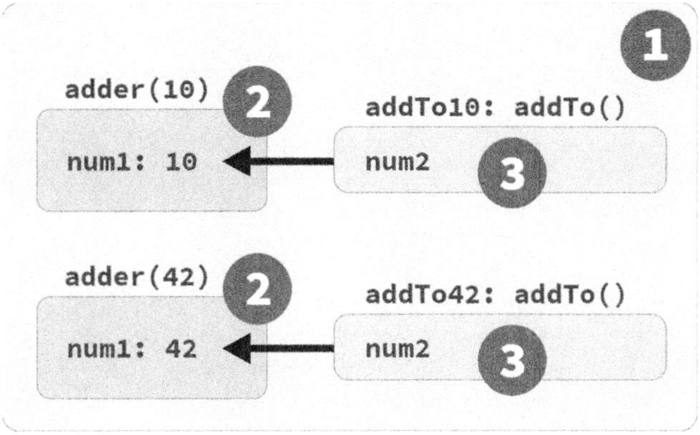

Fig. 4 (repeat): Visualizing Closures

But there's another way of thinking about closure, and more precisely the nature of functions being *passed around*, that may help deepen the mental models.

This alternative model de-emphasizes "functions as first-class values," and instead embraces how functions (like all non-primitive values) are held by reference in JS, and assigned/-passed by reference-copy—see Appendix A of the *Get Started* book for more information.

Instead of thinking about the inner function instance of

addTo(..) moving to the outer RED(1) scope via the return and assignment, we can envision that function instances actually just stay in place in their own scope environment, of course with their scope-chain intact.

What gets *sent* to the RED(1) scope is **just a reference** to the in-place function instance, rather than the function instance itself. Figure 5 depicts the inner function instances remaining in place, pointed to by the RED(1) addTo10 and addTo42 references, respectively:

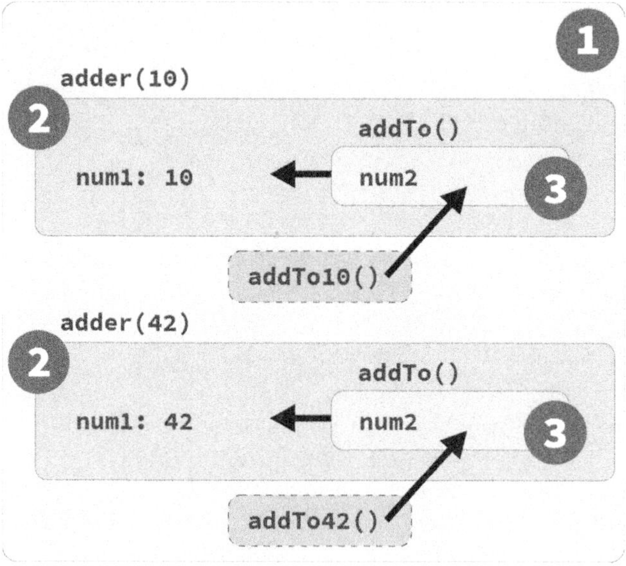

Fig. 5: Visualizing Closures (Alternative)

As shown in Figure 5, each call to adder(..) still creates a new BLUE(2) scope containing a num1 variable, as well as an instance of the GREEN(3) addTo(..) scope. But what's different from Figure 4 is, now these GREEN(3) instances remain in place, naturally nested inside of their BLUE(2) scope instances. The addTo10 and addTo42 references are moved to the RED(1) outer scope, not the function instances themselves.

When `addTo10(15)` is called, the `addTo(..)` function instance (still in place in its original BLUE(2) scope environment) is invoked. Since the function instance itself never moved, of course it still has natural access to its scope chain. Same with the `addTo42(9)` call—nothing special here beyond lexical scope.

So what then *is* closure, if not the *magic* that lets a function maintain a link to its original scope chain even as that function moves around in other scopes? In this alternative model, functions stay in place and keep accessing their original scope chain just like they always could.

Closure instead describes the *magic* of **keeping alive a function instance**, along with its whole scope environment and chain, for as long as there's at least one reference to that function instance floating around in any other part of the program.

That definition of closure is less observational and a bit less familiar-sounding compared to the traditional academic perspective. But it's nonetheless still useful, because the benefit is that we simplify explanation of closure to a straightforward combination of references and in-place function instances.

The previous model (Figure 4) is not *wrong* at describing closure in JS. It's just more conceptually inspired, an academic perspective on closure. By contrast, the alternative model (Figure 5) could be described as a bit more implementation focused, how JS actually works.

Both perspectives/models are useful in understanding closure, but the reader may find one a little easier to hold than the other. Whichever you choose, the observable outcomes in our program are the same.

> **Note**
>
> This alternative model for closure does affect whether we classify synchronous callbacks as examples of closure or not. More on this nuance in Appendix A.

Why Closure?

Now that we have a well-rounded sense of what closure is and how it works, let's explore some ways it can improve the code structure and organization of an example program.

Imagine you have a button on a page that when clicked, should retrieve and send some data via an Ajax request. Without using closure:

```
var APIendpoints = {
    studentIDs:
        "https://some.api/register-students",
    // ..
};

var data = {
    studentIDs: [ 14, 73, 112, 6 ],
    // ..
};

function makeRequest(evt) {
    var btn = evt.target;
```

```
    var recordKind = btn.dataset.kind;
    ajax(
        APIendpoints[recordKind],
        data[recordKind]
    );
}

// <button data-kind="studentIDs">
//    Register Students
// </button>
btn.addEventListener("click",makeRequest);
```

The `makeRequest(..)` utility only receives an `evt` object from a click event. From there, it has to retrieve the `data-kind` attribute from the target button element, and use that value to lookup both a URL for the API endpoint as well as what data should be included in the Ajax request.

This works OK, but it's unfortunate (inefficient, more confusing) that the event handler has to read a DOM attribute each time it's fired. Why couldn't an event handler *remember* this value? Let's try using closure to improve the code:

```
var APIendpoints = {
    studentIDs:
        "https://some.api/register-students",
    // ..
};

var data = {
    studentIDs: [ 14, 73, 112, 6 ],
    // ..
};

function setupButtonHandler(btn) {
    var recordKind = btn.dataset.kind;
```

```
    btn.addEventListener(
        "click",
        function makeRequest(evt){
            ajax(
                APIendpoints[recordKind],
                data[recordKind]
            );
        }
    );
}

// <button data-kind="studentIDs">
//    Register Students
// </button>

setupButtonHandler(btn);
```

With the `setupButtonHandler(..)` approach, the `data-kind` attribute is retrieved once and assigned to the `recordKind` variable at initial setup. `recordKind` is then closed over by the inner `makeRequest(..)` click handler, and its value is used on each event firing to look up the URL and data that should be sent.

Note

`evt` is still passed to `makeRequest(..)`, though in this case we're not using it anymore. It's still listed, for consistency with the previous snippet.

By placing `recordKind` inside `setupButtonHandler(..)`, we limit the scope exposure of that variable to a more appropriate subset of the program; storing it globally would have been worse for code organization and readability. Closure lets the inner `makeRequest()` function instance *remember* this variable and access whenever it's needed.

Building on this pattern, we could have looked up both the URL and data once, at setup:

```
function setupButtonHandler(btn) {
    var recordKind = btn.dataset.kind;
    var requestURL = APIendpoints[recordKind];
    var requestData = data[recordKind];

    btn.addEventListener(
        "click",
        function makeRequest(evt){
            ajax(requestURL,requestData);
        }
    );
}
```

Now `makeRequest(..)` is closed over `requestURL` and `requestData`, which is a little bit cleaner to understand, and also slightly more performant.

Two similar techniques from the Functional Programming (FP) paradigm that rely on closure are partial application and currying. Briefly, with these techniques, we alter the *shape* of functions that require multiple inputs so some inputs are provided up front, and other inputs are provided later; the initial inputs are remembered via closure. Once all inputs have been provided, the underlying action is performed.

By creating a function instance that encapsulates some information inside (via closure), the function-with-stored-information can later be used directly without needing to re-provide that input. This makes that part of the code cleaner, and also offers the opportunity to label partially applied functions with better semantic names.

Adapting partial application, we can further improve the preceding code:

```
function defineHandler(requestURL,requestData) {
    return function makeRequest(evt){
        ajax(requestURL,requestData);
    };
}

function setupButtonHandler(btn) {
    var recordKind = btn.dataset.kind;
    var handler = defineHandler(
        APIendpoints[recordKind],
        data[recordKind]
    );
    btn.addEventListener("click",handler);
}
```

The `requestURL` and `requestData` inputs are provided ahead of time, resulting in the `makeRequest(..)` partially applied function, which we locally label `handler`. When the event eventually fires, the final input (`evt`, even though it's ignored) is passed to `handler()`, completing its inputs and triggering the underlying Ajax request.

Behavior-wise, this program is pretty similar to the previous one, with the same type of closure. But by isolating the creation of `makeRequest(..)` in a separate utility (`defineHandler(..)`), we make that definition more reusable across the program. We also explicitly limit the closure scope to only the two variables needed.

Closer to Closure

As we close down a dense chapter, take some deep breaths let it all sink in. Seriously, that's a lot of information for anyone to consume!

We explored two models for mentally tackling closure:

- Observational: closure is a function instance remembering its outer variables even as that function is passed to and **invoked in** other scopes.
- Implementational: closure is a function instance and its scope environment preserved in-place while any references to it are passed around and **invoked from** other scopes.

Summarizing the benefits to our programs:

- Closure can improve efficiency by allowing a function instance to remember previously determined information instead of having to compute it each time.
- Closure can improve code readability, bounding scope-exposure by encapsulating variable(s) inside function instances, while still making sure the information in those variables is accessible for future use. The resultant narrower, more specialized function instances are cleaner to interact with, since the preserved information doesn't need to be passed in every invocation.

Before you move on, take some time to restate this summary *in your own words*, explaining what closure is and why it's helpful in your programs. The main book text concludes with a final chapter that builds on top of closure with the module pattern.

Chapter 8: The Module Pattern

In this chapter, we wrap up the main text of the book by exploring one of the most important code organization patterns in all of programming: the module. As we'll see, modules are inherently built from what we've already covered: the payoff for your efforts in learning lexical scope and closure.

We've examined every angle of lexical scope, from the breadth of the global scope down through nested block scopes, into the intricacies of the variable lifecycle. Then we leveraged lexical scope to understand the full power of closure.

Take a moment to reflect on how far you've come in this journey so far; you've taken big steps in getting to know JS more deeply!

The central theme of this book has been that understanding and mastering scope and closure is key in properly structuring and organizing our code, especially the decisions on where to store information in variables.

Our goal in this final chapter is to appreciate how modules embody the importance of these topics, elevating them from abstract concepts to concrete, practical improvements in building programs.

Encapsulation and Least Exposure (POLE)

Encapsulation is often cited as a principle of object-oriented (OO) programming, but it's more fundamental and broadly applicable than that. The goal of encapsulation is the bundling or co-location of information (data) and behavior (functions) that together serve a common purpose.

Independent of any syntax or code mechanisms, the spirit of encapsulation can be realized in something as simple as using separate files to hold bits of the overall program with common purpose. If we bundle everything that powers a list of search results into a single file called "search-list.js", we're encapsulating that part of the program.

The recent trend in modern front-end programming to organize applications around Component architecture pushes encapsulation even further. For many, it feels natural to consolidate everything that constitutes the search results list—even beyond code, including presentational markup and styling—into a single unit of program logic, something tangible we can interact with. And then we label that collection the "SearchList" component.

Another key goal is the control of visibility of certain aspects of the encapsulated data and functionality. Recall from Chapter 6 the *least exposure* principle (POLE), which seeks to defensively guard against various *dangers* of scope over-exposure; these affect both variables and functions. In JS, we most often implement visibility control through the mechanics of lexical scope.

The idea is to group alike program bits together, and selectively limit programmatic access to the parts we consider *private* details. What's not considered *private* is then marked as *public*, accessible to the whole program.

The natural effect of this effort is better code organization. It's easier to build and maintain software when we know where things are, with clear and obvious boundaries and connection points. It's also easier to maintain quality if we avoid the pitfalls of over-exposed data and functionality.

These are some of the main benefits of organizing JS programs into modules.

What Is a Module?

A module is a collection of related data and functions (often referred to as methods in this context), characterized by a division between hidden *private* details and *public* accessible details, usually called the "public API."

A module is also stateful: it maintains some information over time, along with functionality to access and update that information.

> **Note**
>
> A broader concern of the module pattern is fully embracing system-level modularization through loose-coupling and other program architecture techniques. That's a complex topic well beyond the bounds of our discussion, but is worth further study beyond this book.

To get a better sense of what a module is, let's compare some module characteristics to useful code patterns that aren't quite modules.

Namespaces (Stateless Grouping)

If you group a set of related functions together, without data, then you don't really have the expected encapsulation a module implies. The better term for this grouping of *stateless* functions is a namespace:

```
// namespace, not module
var Utils = {
    cancelEvt(evt) {
        evt.preventDefault();
        evt.stopPropagation();
        evt.stopImmediatePropagation();
    },
    wait(ms) {
        return new Promise(function c(res){
            setTimeout(res,ms);
        });
    },
    isValidEmail(email) {
        return /[^@]+@[^@.]+\.[^@.]+/.test(email);
    }
};
```

`Utils` here is a useful collection of utilities, yet they're all state-independent functions. Gathering functionality together is generally good practice, but that doesn't make this a module. Rather, we've defined a `Utils` namespace and organized the functions under it.

Data Structures (Stateful Grouping)

Even if you bundle data and stateful functions together, if you're not limiting the visibility of any of it, then you're stopping short of the POLE aspect of encapsulation; it's not particularly helpful to label that a module.

Consider:

```
// data structure, not module
var Student = {
    records: [
        { id: 14, name: "Kyle", grade: 86 },
        { id: 73, name: "Suzy", grade: 87 },
        { id: 112, name: "Frank", grade: 75 },
        { id: 6, name: "Sarah", grade: 91 }
    ],
    getName(studentID) {
        var student = this.records.find(
            student => student.id == studentID
        );
        return student.name;
    }
};

Student.getName(73);
// Suzy
```

Since `records` is publicly accessible data, not hidden behind a public API, `Student` here isn't really a module.

`Student` does have the data-and-functionality aspect of encapsulation, but not the visibility-control aspect. It's best to label this an instance of a data structure.

Modules (Stateful Access Control)

To embody the full spirit of the module pattern, we not only need grouping and state, but also access control through visibility (private vs. public).

Let's turn `Student` from the previous section into a module. We'll start with a form I call the "classic module," which was originally referred to as the "revealing module" when it first emerged in the early 2000s. Consider:

```
var Student = (function defineStudent(){
    var records = [
        { id: 14, name: "Kyle", grade: 86 },
        { id: 73, name: "Suzy", grade: 87 },
        { id: 112, name: "Frank", grade: 75 },
        { id: 6, name: "Sarah", grade: 91 }
    ];

    var publicAPI = {
        getName
    };

    return publicAPI;

    // ************************

    function getName(studentID) {
        var student = records.find(
            student => student.id == studentID
        );
        return student.name;
    }
})();

Student.getName(73);    // Suzy
```

`Student` is now an instance of a module. It features a public API with a single method: `getName(..)`. This method is able to access the private hidden `records` data.

> **Warning**
>
> I should point out that the explicit student data being hard-coded into this module definition is just for our illustration purposes. A typical module in your program will receive this data from an outside source, typically loaded from databases, JSON data files, Ajax calls, etc. The data is then injected into the module instance typically through method(s) on the module's public API.

How does the classic module format work?

Notice that the instance of the module is created by the `defineStudent()` IIFE being executed. This IIFE returns an object (named `publicAPI`) that has a property on it referencing the inner `getName(..)` function.

Naming the object `publicAPI` is stylistic preference on my part. The object can be named whatever you like (JS doesn't care), or you can just return an object directly without assigning it to any internal named variable. More on this choice in Appendix A.

From the outside, `Student.getName(..)` invokes this exposed inner function, which maintains access to the inner `records` variable via closure.

You don't *have* to return an object with a function as one of its properties. You could just return a function directly, in place of the object. That still satisfies all the core bits of a classic module.

By virtue of how lexical scope works, defining variables and functions inside your outer module definition function makes everything *by default* private. Only properties added to the public API object returned from the function will be exported for external public use.

The use of an IIFE implies that our program only ever needs a single central instance of the module, commonly referred to as a "singleton." Indeed, this specific example is simple enough that there's no obvious reason we'd need anything more than just one instance of the `Student` module.

Module Factory (Multiple Instances)

But if we did want to define a module that supported multiple instances in our program, we can slightly tweak the code:

```
// factory function, not singleton IIFE
function defineStudent() {
    var records = [
        { id: 14, name: "Kyle", grade: 86 },
        { id: 73, name: "Suzy", grade: 87 },
        { id: 112, name: "Frank", grade: 75 },
        { id: 6, name: "Sarah", grade: 91 }
    ];

    var publicAPI = {
        getName
    };

    return publicAPI;

    // ************************

    function getName(studentID) {
```

```
        var student = records.find(
            student => student.id == studentID
        );
        return student.name;
    }
}

var fullTime = defineStudent();
fullTime.getName(73);            // Suzy
```

Rather than specifying `defineStudent()` as an IIFE, we just define it as a normal standalone function, which is commonly referred to in this context as a "module factory" function.

We then call the module factory, producing an instance of the module that we label `fullTime`. This module instance implies a new instance of the inner scope, and thus a new closure that `getName(..)` holds over `records`. `fullTime.getName(..)` now invokes the method on that specific instance.

Classic Module Definition

So to clarify what makes something a classic module:

- There must be an outer scope, typically from a module factory function running at least once.
- The module's inner scope must have at least one piece of hidden information that represents state for the module.
- The module must return on its public API a reference to at least one function that has closure over the hidden module state (so that this state is actually preserved).

You'll likely run across other variations on this classic module approach, which we'll look at in more detail in Appendix A.

Node CommonJS Modules

In Chapter 4, we introduced the CommonJS module format used by Node. Unlike the classic module format described earlier, where you could bundle the module factory or IIFE alongside any other code including other modules, CommonJS modules are file-based; one module per file.

Let's tweak our module example to adhere to that format:

```
module.exports.getName = getName;

// ************************

var records = [
    { id: 14, name: "Kyle", grade: 86 },
    { id: 73, name: "Suzy", grade: 87 },
    { id: 112, name: "Frank", grade: 75 },
    { id: 6, name: "Sarah", grade: 91 }
];

function getName(studentID) {
    var student = records.find(
        student => student.id == studentID
    );
    return student.name;
}
```

The `records` and `getName` identifiers are in the top-level scope of this module, but that's not the global scope (as explained in Chapter 4). As such, everything here is *by default* private to the module.

To expose something on the public API of a CommonJS module, you add a property to the empty object provided as `module.exports`. In some older legacy code, you may run across references to just a bare `exports`, but for code clarity you should always fully qualify that reference with the `module.` prefix.

For style purposes, I like to put my "exports" at the top and my module implementation at the bottom. But these exports can be placed anywhere. I strongly recommend collecting them all together, either at the top or bottom of your file.

Some developers have the habit of replacing the default exports object, like this:

```
// defining a new object for the API
module.exports = {
    // ..exports..
};
```

There are some quirks with this approach, including unexpected behavior if multiple such modules circularly depend on each other. As such, I recommend against replacing the object. If you want to assign multiple exports at once, using object literal style definition, you can do this instead:

```
Object.assign(module.exports,{
   // .. exports ..
});
```

What's happening here is defining the `{ .. }` object literal with your module's public API specified, and then `Object.assign(..)` is performing a shallow copy of all those properties onto the existing `module.exports` object, instead of replacing it This is a nice balance of convenience and safer module behavior.

To include another module instance into your module/program, use Node's `require(..)` method. Assuming this module is located at "/path/to/student.js", this is how we can access it:

```
var Student = require("/path/to/student.js");

Student.getName(73);
// Suzy
```

`Student` now references the public API of our example module.

CommonJS modules behave as singleton instances, similar to the IIFE module definition style presented before. No matter how many times you `require(..)` the same module, you just get additional references to the single shared module instance.

`require(..)` is an all-or-nothing mechanism; it includes a reference of the entire exposed public API of the module. To effectively access only part of the API, the typical approach looks like this:

```
var getName = require("/path/to/student.js").getName;

// or alternately:

var { getName } = require("/path/to/student.js");
```

Similar to the classic module format, the publicly exported methods of a CommonJS module's API hold closures over the internal module details. That's how the module singleton state is maintained across the lifetime of your program.

Note

In Node `require("student")` statements, non-absolute paths (`"student"`) assume a ".js" file extension and search "node_modules".

Modern ES Modules (ESM)

The ESM format shares several similarities with the CommonJS format. ESM is file-based, and module instances are singletons, with everything private *by default*. One notable difference is that ESM files are assumed to be strict-mode, without needing a `"use strict"` pragma at the top. There's no way to define an ESM as non-strict-mode.

Instead of `module.exports` in CommonJS, ESM uses an `export` keyword to expose something on the public API of the module. The `import` keyword replaces the `require(..)` statement. Let's adjust "students.js" to use the ESM format:

```
export { getName };

// ************************

var records = [
    { id: 14, name: "Kyle", grade: 86 },
    { id: 73, name: "Suzy", grade: 87 },
    { id: 112, name: "Frank", grade: 75 },
    { id: 6, name: "Sarah", grade: 91 }
];

function getName(studentID) {
    var student = records.find(
```

```
        student => student.id == studentID
    );
    return student.name;
}
```

The only change here is the `export { getName }` statement. As before, `export` statements can appear anywhere throughout the file, though `export` must be at the top-level scope; it cannot be inside any other block or function.

ESM offers a fair bit of variation on how the `export` statements can be specified. For example:

```
export function getName(studentID) {
    // ..
}
```

Even though `export` appears before the `function` keyword here, this form is still a `function` declaration that also happens to be exported. That is, the `getName` identifier is *function hoisted* (see Chapter 5), so it's available throughout the whole scope of the module.

Another allowed variation:

```
export default function getName(studentID) {
    // ..
}
```

This is a so-called "default export," which has different semantics from other exports. In essence, a "default export" is a shorthand for consumers of the module when they `import`, giving them a terser syntax when they only need this single default API member.

Non-`default` exports are referred to as "named exports."

The `import` keyword—like `export`, it must be used only at the top level of an ESM outside of any blocks or functions—also has a number of variations in syntax. The first is referred to as "named import":

```
import { getName } from "/path/to/students.js";

getName(73);    // Suzy
```

As you can see, this form imports only the specifically named public API members from a module (skipping anything not named explicitly), and it adds those identifiers to the top-level scope of the current module. This type of import is a familiar style to those used to package imports in languages like Java.

Multiple API members can be listed inside the `{ .. }` set, separated with commas. A named import can also be *renamed* with the as keyword:

```
import { getName as getStudentName }
   from "/path/to/students.js";

getStudentName(73);    // Suzy
```

If `getName` is a "default export" of the module, we can import it like this:

```
import getName from "/path/to/students.js";

getName(73);    // Suzy
```

The only difference here is dropping the `{ }` around the import binding. If you want to mix a default import with other named imports:

```
import { default as getName, /* .. others .. */ }
   from "/path/to/students.js";

getName(73);   // Suzy
```

By contrast, the other major variation on `import` is called "namespace import":

```
import * as Student from "/path/to/students.js";

Student.getName(73);   // Suzy
```

As is likely obvious, the `*` imports everything exported to the API, default and named, and stores it all under the single namespace identifier as specified. This approach most closely matches the form of classic modules for most of JS's history.

> **Note**
>
> As of the time of this writing, modern browsers have supported ESM for a few years now, but Node's stable'ish support for ESM is fairly recent, and has been evolving for quite a while. The evolution is likely to continue for another year or more; the introduction of ESM to JS back in ES6 created a number of challenging compatibility concerns for Node's interop with CommonJS modules. Consult Node's ESM documentation for all the latest details: https://nodejs.org/api/esm.html

Exit Scope

Whether you use the classic module format (browser or Node), CommonJS format (in Node), or ESM format (browser or Node), modules are one of the most effective ways to structure and organize your program's functionality and data.

The module pattern is the conclusion of our journey in this book of learning how we can use the rules of lexical scope to place variables and functions in proper locations. POLE is the defensive *private by default* posture we always take, making sure we avoid over-exposure and interact only with the minimal public API surface area necessary.

And underneath modules, the *magic* of how all our module state is maintained is closures leveraging the lexical scope system.

That's it for the main text. Congratulations on quite a journey so far! As I've said numerous times throughout, it's a really good idea to pause, reflect, and practice what we've just discussed.

When you're comfortable and ready, check out the appendices, which dig deeper into some of the corners of these topics, and also challenge you with some practice exercises to solidify what you've learned.

Appendix A: Exploring Further

We will now explore a number of nuances and edges around many of the topics covered in the main text of this book. This appendix is optional, supporting material.

Some people find diving too deeply into the nuanced corner cases and varying opinions creates nothing but noise and distraction—supposedly, developers are better served by sticking to the commonly-tread paths. My approach has been criticized as being impractical and counterproductive. I understand and appreciate that perspective, even if I don't necessarily share it.

I believe it's better to be empowered by knowledge of how things work than to just gloss over details with assumptions and lack of curiosity. Ultimately, you will encounter situations where something bubbles up from a piece you hadn't explored. In other words, you won't get to spend all your time riding on the smooth *happy path*. Wouldn't you rather be prepared for the inevitable bumps of off-roading?

These discussions will also be more heavily influenced by my opinions than the main text was, so keep that in mind as you consume and consider what is presented. This appendix is a bit like a collection of mini-blog posts that elaborate on various book topics. It's long and deep in the weeds, so take your time and don't rush through everything here.

Implied Scopes

Scopes are sometimes created in non-obvious places. In practice, these implied scopes don't often impact your program behavior, but it's still useful to know they're happening. Keep an eye out for the following surprising scopes:

- Parameter scope
- Function name scope

Parameter Scope

The conversation metaphor in Chapter 2 implies that function parameters are basically the same as locally declared variables in the function scope. But that's not always true.

Consider:

```
// outer/global scope: RED(1)

function getStudentName(studentID) {
    // function scope: BLUE(2)

    // ..
}
```

Here, `studentID` is a considered a "simple" parameter, so it does behave as a member of the BLUE(2) function scope. But if we change it to be a non-simple parameter, that's no longer technically the case. Parameter forms considered non-simple include parameters with default values, rest parameters (using `...`), and destructured parameters.

Consider:

```
// outer/global scope: RED(1)

function getStudentName(/*BLUE(2)*/ studentID = 0) {
    // function scope: GREEN(3)

    // ..
}
```

Here, the parameter list essentially becomes its own scope, and the function's scope is then nested inside *that* scope.

Why? What difference does it make? The non-simple parameter forms introduce various corner cases, so the parameter list becomes its own scope to more effectively deal with them.

Consider:

```
function getStudentName(studentID = maxID, maxID) {
    // ..
}
```

Assuming left-to-right operations, the default `= maxID` for the `studentID` parameter requires a `maxID` to already exist (and to have been initialized). This code produces a TDZ error (Chapter 5). The reason is that `maxID` is declared in the parameter scope, but it's not yet been initialized because of the order of parameters. If the parameter order is flipped, no TDZ error occurs:

```
function getStudentName(maxID,studentID = maxID) {
    // ..
}
```

The complication gets even more *in the weeds* if we introduce a function expression into the default parameter position, which then can create its own closure (Chapter 7) over parameters in this implied parameter scope:

```
function whatsTheDealHere(id,defaultID = () => id) {
    id = 5;
    console.log( defaultID() );
}

whatsTheDealHere(3);
// 5
```

That snippet probably makes sense, because the `defaultID()` arrow function closes over the `id` parameter/variable, which we then re-assign to `5`. But now let's introduce a shadowing definition of `id` in the function scope:

```
function whatsTheDealHere(id,defaultID = () => id) {
    var id = 5;
    console.log( defaultID() );
}

whatsTheDealHere(3);
// 3
```

Uh oh! The `var id = 5` is shadowing the `id` parameter, but the closure of the `defaultID()` function is over the parameter, not the shadowing variable in the function body. This proves there's a scope bubble around the parameter list.

But it gets even crazier than that!

```
function whatsTheDealHere(id,defaultID = () => id) {
    var id;

    console.log(`local variable 'id': ${ id }`);
    console.log(
        `parameter 'id' (closure): ${ defaultID() }`
    );

    console.log("reassigning 'id' to 5");
    id = 5;

    console.log(`local variable 'id': ${ id }`);
    console.log(
        `parameter 'id' (closure): ${ defaultID() }`
    );
}

whatsTheDealHere(3);
// local variable 'id': 3   <--- Huh!? Weird!
// parameter 'id' (closure): 3
// reassigning 'id' to 5
// local variable 'id': 5
// parameter 'id' (closure): 3
```

The strange bit here is the first console message. At that moment, the shadowing `id` local variable has just been `var id` declared, which Chapter 5 asserts is typically auto-initialized to `undefined` at the top of its scope. Why doesn't it print `undefined`?

In this specific corner case (for legacy compat reasons), JS doesn't auto-initialize `id` to `undefined`, but rather to the value of the `id` parameter (`3`)!

Though the two `id`s look at that moment like they're one variable, they're actually still separate (and in separate scopes).

The `id = 5` assignment makes the divergence observable, where the `id` parameter stays `3` and the local variable becomes `5`.

My advice to avoid getting bitten by these weird nuances:

- Never shadow parameters with local variables
- Avoid using a default parameter function that closes over any of the parameters

At least now you're aware and can be careful about the fact that the parameter list is its own scope if any of the parameters are non-simple.

Function Name Scope

In the "Function Name Scope" section in Chapter 3, I asserted that the name of a function expression is added to the function's own scope. Recall:

```
var askQuestion = function ofTheTeacher(){
    // ..
};
```

It's true that `ofTheTeacher` is not added to the enclosing scope (where `askQuestion` is declared), but it's also not *just* added to the scope of the function, the way you're likely assuming. It's another strange corner case of implied scope.

The name identifier of a function expression is in its own implied scope, nested between the outer enclosing scope and the main inner function scope.

If `ofTheTeacher` was in the function's scope, we'd expect an error here:

```
var askQuestion = function ofTheTeacher(){
    // why is this not a duplicate declaration error?
    let ofTheTeacher = "Confused, yet?";
};
```

The `let` declaration form does not allow re-declaration (see Chapter 5). But this is perfectly legal shadowing, not re-declaration, because the two `ofTheTeacher` identifiers are in separate scopes.

You'll rarely run into any case where the scope of a function's name identifier matters. But again, it's good to know how these mechanisms actually work. To avoid being bitten, never shadow function name identifiers.

Anonymous vs. Named Functions

As discussed in Chapter 3, functions can be expressed either in named or anonymous form. It's vastly more common to use the anonymous form, but is that a good idea?

As you contemplate naming your functions, consider:

- Name inference is incomplete
- Lexical names allow self-reference
- Names are useful descriptions
- Arrow functions have no lexical names
- IIFEs also need names

Explicit or Inferred Names?

Every function in your program has a purpose. If it doesn't have a purpose, take it out, because you're just wasting space. If it *does* have a purpose, there *is* a name for that purpose.

So far many readers likely agree with me. But does that mean we should always put that name into the code? Here's where I'll raise more than a few eyebrows. I say, unequivocally, yes!

First of all, "anonymous" showing up in stack traces is just not all that helpful to debugging:

```
btn.addEventListener("click",function(){
    setTimeout(function(){
        ["a",42].map(function(v){
            console.log(v.toUpperCase());
        });
    },100);
});
// Uncaught TypeError: v.toUpperCase is not a function
//     at myProgram.js:4
//     at Array.map (<anonymous>)
//     at myProgram.js:3
```

Ugh. Compare to what is reported if I give the functions names:

```
btn.addEventListener("click",function onClick(){
    setTimeout(function waitAMoment(){
        ["a",42].map(function allUpper(v){
            console.log(v.toUpperCase());
        });
    },100);
});
// Uncaught TypeError: v.toUpperCase is not a function
//     at allUpper (myProgram.js:4)
//     at Array.map (<anonymous>)
//     at waitAMoment (myProgram.js:3)
```

See how waitAMoment and allUpper names appear and give the stack trace more useful information/context for debugging? The program is more debuggable if we use reasonable names for all our functions.

Note

The unfortunate "<anonymous>" that still shows up refers to the fact that the implementation of Array.map(..) isn't present in our program, but is built into the JS engine. It's not from any confusion our program introduces with readability shortcuts.

By the way, let's make sure we're on the same page about what a named function is:

```
function thisIsNamed() {
    // ..
}

ajax("some.url",function thisIsAlsoNamed(){
   // ..
});

var notNamed = function(){
    // ..
};

makeRequest({
    data: 42,
    cb /* also not a name */: function(){
        // ..
    }
});
```

```
var stillNotNamed = function butThisIs(){
    // ..
};
```

"But wait!", you say. Some of those *are* named, right!?

```
var notNamed = function(){
    // ..
};

var config = {
    cb: function(){
        // ..
    }
};

notNamed.name;
// notNamed

config.cb.name;
// cb
```

These are referred to as *inferred* names. Inferred names are fine, but they don't really address the full concern I'm discussing.

Missing Names?

Yes, these inferred names might show up in stack traces, which is definitely better than "anonymous" showing up. But...

```
function ajax(url,cb) {
    console.log(cb.name);
}

ajax("some.url",function(){
    // ..
});
// ""
```

Oops. Anonymous `function` expressions passed as callbacks are incapable of receiving an inferred name, so `cb.name` holds just the empty string `""`. The vast majority of all `function` expressions, especially anonymous ones, are used as callback arguments; none of these get a name. So relying on name inference is incomplete, at best.

And it's not just callbacks that fall short with inference:

```
var config = {};

config.cb = function(){
    // ..
};

config.cb.name;
// ""

var [ noName ] = [ function(){} ];
noName.name
// ""
```

Any assignment of a `function` expression that's not a *simple assignment* will also fail name inferencing. So, in other words, unless you're careful and intentional about it, essentially almost all anonymous `function` expressions in your program will in fact have no name at all.

Name inference is just... not enough.

And even if a `function` expression *does* get an inferred name, that still doesn't count as being a full named function.

Who am I?

Without a lexical name identifier, the function has no internal way to refer to itself. Self-reference is important for things like recursion and event handling:

```
// broken
runOperation(function(num){
    if (num <= 1) return 1;
    return num * oopsNoNameToCall(num - 1);
});

// also broken
btn.addEventListener("click",function(){
   console.log("should only respond to one click!");
   btn.removeEventListener("click",oopsNoNameHere);
});
```

Leaving off the lexical name from your callback makes it harder to reliably self-reference the function. You *could* declare a variable in an enclosing scope that references the function, but this variable is *controlled* by that enclosing scope—it could be re-assigned, etc.—so it's not as reliable as the function having its own internal self-reference.

Names are Descriptors

Lastly, and I think most importantly of all, leaving off a name from a function makes it harder for the reader to tell what the function's purpose is, at a quick glance. They have to read more of the code, including the code inside the function, and the surrounding code outside the function, to figure it out.

Consider:

```
[ 1, 2, 3, 4, 5 ].filter(function(v){
    return v % 2 == 1;
});
// [ 1, 3, 5 ]

[ 1, 2, 3, 4, 5 ].filter(function keepOnlyOdds(v){
    return v % 2 == 1;
});
// [ 1, 3, 5 ]
```

There's just no reasonable argument to be made that **omitting** the name `keepOnlyOdds` from the first callback more effectively communicates to the reader the purpose of this callback. You saved 13 characters, but lost important readability information. The name `keepOnlyOdds` very clearly tells the reader, at a quick first glance, what's happening.

The JS engine doesn't care about the name. But human readers of your code absolutely do.

Can the reader look at `v % 2 == 1` and figure out what it's doing? Sure. But they have to infer the purpose (and name) by mentally executing the code. Even a brief pause to do so slows down reading of the code. A good descriptive name makes this process almost effortless and instant.

Think of it this way: how many times does the author of this code need to figure out the purpose of a function before adding the name to the code? About once. Maybe two or three times if they need to adjust the name. But how many times will readers of this code have to figure out the name/purpose? Every single time this line is ever read. Hundreds of times? Thousands? More?

No matter the length or complexity of the function, my assertion is, the author should figure out a good descriptive name and add it to the code. Even the one-liner functions in `map(..)` and `then(..)` statements should be named:

```
lookupTheRecords(someData)
.then(function extractSalesRecords(resp){
   return resp.allSales;
})
.then(storeRecords);
```

The name `extractSalesRecords` tells the reader the purpose of this `then(..)` handler *better* than just inferring that purpose from mentally executing `return resp.allSales`.

The only excuse for not including a name on a function is either laziness (don't want to type a few extra characters) or uncreativity (can't come up with a good name). If you can't figure out a good name, you likely don't understand the function and its purpose yet. The function is perhaps poorly designed, or it does too many things, and should be re-worked. Once you have a well-designed, single-purpose function, its proper name should become evident.

Here's a trick I use: while first writing a function, if I don't fully understand its purpose and can't think of a good name to use, I just use `TODO` as the name. That way, later when reviewing my code, I'm likely to find those name placeholders, and I'm more inclined (and more prepared!) to go back and figure out a better name, rather than just leave it as `TODO`.

All functions need names. Every single one. No exceptions. Any name you omit is making the program harder to read, harder to debug, harder to extend and maintain later.

Arrow Functions

Arrow functions are **always** anonymous, even if (rarely) they're used in a way that gives them an inferred name. I just spent several pages explaining why anonymous functions are a bad idea, so you can probably guess what I think about arrow functions.

Don't use them as a general replacement for regular functions. They're more concise, yes, but that brevity comes at the cost of omitting key visual delimiters that help our brains quickly parse out what we're reading. And, to the point of this discussion, they're anonymous, which makes them worse for readability from that angle as well.

Arrow functions have a purpose, but that purpose is not to save keystrokes. Arrow functions have *lexical this* behavior, which is somewhat beyond the bounds of our discussion in this book.

Briefly: arrow functions don't define a `this` identifier keyword at all. If you use a `this` inside an arrow function, it behaves exactly as any other variable reference, which is that the scope chain is consulted to find a function scope (non-arrow function) where it *is* defined, and to use that one.

In other words, arrow functions treat `this` like any other lexical variable.

If you're used to hacks like `var self = this`, or if you prefer to call `.bind(this)` on inner `function` expressions, just to force them to inherit a `this` from an outer function like it was a lexical variable, then => arrow functions are absolutely the better option. They're designed specifically to fix that problem.

So, in the rare cases you need *lexical this*, use an arrow function. It's the best tool for that job. But just be aware that in doing so, you're accepting the downsides of an anonymous function. You should expend additional effort to mitigate the readability *cost*, such as more descriptive variable names and code comments.

IIFE Variations

All functions should have names. I said that a few times, right!? That includes IIFEs.

```
(function(){
    // don't do this!
})();

(function doThisInstead(){
    // ..
})();
```

How do we come up with a name for an IIFE? Identify what the IIFE is there for. Why do you need a scope in that spot? Are you hiding a cache variable for student records?

```
var getStudents = (function StoreStudentRecords(){
    var studentRecords = [];

    return function getStudents() {
        // ..
    }
})();
```

I named the IIFE `StoreStudentRecords` because that's what it's doing: storing student records. Every IIFE should have a name. No exceptions.

IIFEs are typically defined by placing `( .. )` around the `function` expression, as shown in those previous snippets. But that's not the only way to define an IIFE. Technically, the only reason we're using that first surrounding set of `( .. )` is just so the `function` keyword isn't in a position to qualify as a `function` declaration to the JS parser. But there are other syntactic ways to avoid being parsed as a declaration:

```
!function thisIsAnIIFE(){
    // ..
}();

+function soIsThisOne(){
    // ..
}();

~function andThisOneToo(){
    // ..
}();
```

The `!`, `+`, `~`, and several other unary operators (operators with one operand) can all be placed in front of `function` to turn it into an expression. Then the final `()` call is valid, which makes it an IIFE.

I actually kind of like using the `void` unary operator when defining a standalone IIFE:

```
void function yepItsAnIIFE() {
    // ..
}();
```

The benefit of `void` is, it clearly communicates at the beginning of the function that this IIFE won't be returning any value.

However you define your IIFEs, show them some love by giving them names.

Hoisting: Functions and Variables

Chapter 5 articulated both *function hoisting* and *variable hoisting*. Since hoisting is often cited as mistake in the design of JS, I wanted to briefly explore why both these forms of hoisting *can* be beneficial and should still be considered.

Give hoisting a deeper level of consideration by considering the merits of:

- Executable code first, function declarations last
- Semantic placement of variable declarations

Function Hoisting

To review, this program works because of *function hoisting*:

```
getStudents();

// ..

function getStudents() {
    // ..
}
```

The `function` declaration is hoisted during compilation, which means that `getStudents` is an identifier declared for the entire scope. Additionally, the `getStudents` identifier is auto-initialized with the function reference, again at the beginning of the scope.

Why is this useful? The reason I prefer to take advantage of *function hoisting* is that it puts the *executable* code in any scope at the top, and any further declarations (functions) below. This means it's easier to find the code that will run in any given area, rather than having to scroll and scroll, hoping to find a trailing } marking the end of a scope/function somewhere.

I take advantage of this inverse positioning in all levels of scope:

```
getStudents();

// *************

function getStudents() {
    var whatever = doSomething();

    // other stuff

    return whatever;
```

```
    // *************

    function doSomething() {
        // ..
    }
}
```

When I first open a file like that, the very first line is executable code that kicks off its behavior. That's very easy to spot! Then, if I ever need to go find and inspect `getStudents()`, I like that its first line is also executable code. Only if I need to see the details of `doSomething()` do I go and find its definition down below.

In other words, I think *function hoisting* makes code more readable through a flowing, progressive reading order, from top to bottom.

Variable Hoisting

What about *variable hoisting*?

Even though `let` and `const` hoist, you cannot use those variables in their TDZ (see Chapter 5). So, the following discussion only applies to `var` declarations. Before I continue, I'll admit: in almost all cases, I completely agree that *variable hoisting* is a bad idea:

```
pleaseDontDoThis = "bad idea";

// much later
var pleaseDontDoThis;
```

While that kind of inverted ordering was helpful for *function hoisting*, here I think it usually makes code harder to reason about.

But there's one exception that I've found, somewhat rarely, in my own coding. It has to do with where I place my `var` declarations inside a CommonJS module definition.

Here's how I typically structure my module definitions in Node:

```
// dependencies
var aModuleINeed = require("very-helpful");
var anotherModule = require("kinda-helpful");

// public API
var publicAPI = Object.assign(module.exports,{
    getStudents,
    addStudents,
    // ..
});

// ********************************
// private implementation

var cache = { };
var otherData = [ ];

function getStudents() {
    // ..
}

function addStudents() {
    // ..
}
```

Notice how the `cache` and `otherData` variables are in the "private" section of the module layout? That's because I don't plan to expose them publicly. So I organize the module so they're located alongside the other hidden implementation details of the module.

But I've had a few rare cases where I needed the assignments of those values to happen *above*, before I declare the exported public API of the module. For instance:

```
// public API
var publicAPI = Object.assign(module.exports,{
    getStudents,
    addStudents,
    refreshData: refreshData.bind(null,cache)
});
```

I need the `cache` variable to have already been assigned a value, because that value is used in the initialization of the public API (the `.bind(..)` partial-application).

Should I just move the `var cache = { .. }` up to the top, above this public API initialization? Well, perhaps. But now it's less obvious that `var cache` is a *private* implementation detail. Here's the compromise I've (somewhat rarely) used:

```
cache = {};   // used here, but declared below

// public API
var publicAPI = Object.assign(module.exports,{
    getStudents,
    addStudents,
    refreshData: refreshData.bind(null,cache)
});

// ********************************
// private implementation

var cache /* = {}*/;
```

See the *variable hoisting*? I've declared the `cache` down where it belongs, logically, but in this rare case I've used it earlier up above, in the area where its initialization is needed. I even left a hint at the value that's assigned to `cache` in a code comment.

That's literally the only case I've ever found for leveraging *variable hoisting* to assign a variable earlier in a scope than its declaration. But I think it's a reasonable exception to employ with caution.

The Case for `var`

Speaking of *variable hoisting*, let's have some real talk for a bit about `var`, a favorite villain devs love to blame for many of the woes of JS development. In Chapter 5, we explored `let`/`const` and promised we'd revisit where `var` falls in the whole mix.

As I lay out the case, don't miss:

- `var` was never broken
- `let` is your friend
- `const` has limited utility
- The best of both worlds: `var` *and* `let`

Don't Throw Out `var`

`var` is fine, and works just fine. It's been around for 25 years, and it'll be around and useful and functional for another 25 years or more. Claims that `var` is broken, deprecated, outdated, dangerous, or ill-designed are bogus bandwagoning.

Does that mean `var` is the right declarator for every single declaration in your program? Certainly not. But it still has its place in your programs. Refusing to use it because someone on the team chose an aggressive linter opinion that chokes on `var` is cutting off your nose to spite your face.

OK, now that I've got you really riled up, let me try to explain my position.

For the record, I'm a fan of `let`, for block-scoped declarations. I really dislike TDZ and I think that was a mistake. But `let` itself is great. I use it often. In fact, I probably use it as much or more than I use `var`.

`const`-antly Confused

`const` on the other hand, I don't use as often. I'm not going to dig into all the reasons why, but it comes down to `const` not *carrying its own weight*. That is, while there's a tiny bit of benefit of `const` in some cases, that benefit is outweighed by the long history of troubles around `const` confusion in a variety of languages, long before it ever showed up in JS.

`const` pretends to create values that can't be mutated—a misconception that's extremely common in developer communities across many languages—whereas what it really does is prevent re-assignment.

```
const studentIDs = [ 14, 73, 112 ];

// later

studentIDs.push(6);   // whoa, wait... what!?
```

Using a `const` with a mutable value (like an array or object) is asking for a future developer (or reader of your code) to fall into the trap you set, which was that they either didn't know, or sorta forgot, that *value immutability* isn't at all the same thing as *assignment immutability*.

I just don't think we should set those traps. The only time I ever use `const` is when I'm assigning an already-immutable value (like `42` or `"Hello, friends!"`), and when it's clearly a "constant" in the sense of being a named placeholder for a literal value, for semantic purposes. That's what `const` is best used for. That's pretty rare in my code, though.

If variable re-assignment were a big deal, then `const` would be more useful. But variable re-assignment just isn't that big of a deal in terms of causing bugs. There's a long list of things that lead to bugs in programs, but "accidental re-assignment" is way, way down that list.

Combine that with the fact that `const` (and `let`) are supposed to be used in blocks, and blocks are supposed to be short, and you have a really small area of your code where a `const` declaration is even applicable. A `const` on line `1` of your ten-line block only tells you something about the next nine lines. And the thing it tells you is already obvious by glancing down at those nine lines: the variable is never on the left-hand side of an =; it's not re-assigned.

That's it, that's all `const` really does. Other than that, it's not very useful. Stacked up against the significant confusion of value vs. assignment immutability, `const` loses a lot of its luster.

A `let` (or `var`!) that's never re-assigned is already behaviorally a "constant", even though it doesn't have the compiler guarantee. That's good enough in most cases.

`var` *and* `let`

In my mind, `const` is pretty rarely useful, so this is only two-horse race between `let` and `var`. But it's not really a race either, because there doesn't have to be just one winner. They can both win... different races.

The fact is, you should be using both `var` and `let` in your programs. They are not interchangeable: you shouldn't use `var` where a `let` is called for, but you also shouldn't use `let` where a `var` is most appropriate.

So where should we still use `var`? Under what circumstances is it a better choice than `let`?

For one, I always use `var` in the top-level scope of any function, regardless of whether that's at the beginning, middle, or end of the function. I also use `var` in the global scope, though I try to minimize usage of the global scope.

Why use `var` for function scoping? Because that's exactly what `var` does. There literally is no better tool for the job of function scoping a declaration than a declarator that has, for 25 years, done exactly that.

You *could* use `let` in this top-level scope, but it's not the best tool for that job. I also find that if you use `let` everywhere, then it's less obvious which declarations are designed to be localized and which ones are intended to be used throughout the function.

By contrast, I rarely use a `var` inside a block. That's what `let` is for. Use the best tool for the job. If you see a `let`, it tells you that you're dealing with a localized declaration. If you see `var`, it tells you that you're dealing with a function-wide declaration. Simple as that.

```
function getStudents(data) {
    var studentRecords = [];

    for (let record of data.records) {
        let id = `student-${ record.id }`;
        studentRecords.push({
            id,
            record.name
        });
    }

    return studentRecords;
}
```

The `studentRecords` variable is intended for use across the whole function. `var` is the best declarator to tell the reader that. By contrast, `record` and `id` are intended for use only in the narrower scope of the loop iteration, so `let` is the best tool for that job.

In addition to this *best tool* semantic argument, `var` has a few other characteristics that, in certain limited circumstances, make it more powerful.

One example is when a loop is exclusively using a variable, but its conditional clause cannot see block-scoped declarations inside the iteration:

```
function commitAction() {
    do {
        let result = commit();
        var done = result && result.code == 1;
    } while (!done);
}
```

Here, `result` is clearly only used inside the block, so we use `let`. But `done` is a bit different. It's only useful for the loop, but the `while` clause cannot see `let` declarations that appear inside the loop. So we compromise and use `var`, so that `done` is hoisted to the outer scope where it can be seen.

The alternative—declaring `done` outside the loop—separates it from where it's first used, and either necessitates picking a default value to assign, or worse, leaving it unassigned and thus looking ambiguous to the reader. I think `var` inside the loop is preferable here.

Another helpful characteristic of `var` is seen with declarations inside unintended blocks. Unintended blocks are blocks that are created because the syntax requires a block, but where the intent of the developer is not really to create a localized scope. The best illustration of unintended scope is the `try..catch` statement:

```
function getStudents() {
    try {
        // not really a block scope
        var records = fromCache("students");
    }
    catch (err) {
        // oops, fall back to a default
        var records = [];
    }
    // ..
}
```

There are other ways to structure this code, yes. But I think this is the *best* way, given various trade-offs.

I don't want to declare `records` (with `var` or `let`) outside of the `try` block, and then assign to it in one or both blocks. I prefer initial declarations to always be as close as possible (ideally, same line) to the first usage of the variable. In this simple example, that would only be a couple of lines distance, but in real code it can grow to many more lines. The bigger the gap, the harder it is to figure out what variable from what scope you're assigning to. `var` used at the actual assignment makes it less ambiguous.

Also notice I used `var` in both the `try` and `catch` blocks. That's because I want to signal to the reader that no matter which path is taken, `records` always gets declared. Technically, that works because `var` is hoisted once to the function scope. But it's still a nice semantic signal to remind the reader what either `var` ensures. If `var` were only used in one of the blocks, and you were only reading the other block, you wouldn't as easily discover where `records` was coming from.

This is, in my opinion, a little superpower of `var`. Not only can it escape the unintentional `try..catch` blocks, but it's allowed to appear multiple times in a function's scope. You can't do that with `let`. It's not bad, it's actually a little helpful feature. Think of `var` more like a declarative annotation that's reminding you, each usage, where the variable comes from. "Ah ha, right, it belongs to the whole function."

This repeated-annotation superpower is useful in other cases:

```
function getStudents() {
    var data = [];

    // do something with data
    // .. 50 more lines of code ..

    // purely an annotation to remind us
    var data;

    // use data again
```

```
    // ..
}
```

The second `var data` is not re-declaring `data`, it's just annotating for the readers' benefit that `data` is a function-wide declaration. That way, the reader doesn't need to scroll up 50+ lines of code to find the initial declaration.

I'm perfectly fine with re-using variables for multiple purposes throughout a function scope. I'm also perfectly fine with having two usages of a variable be separated by quite a few lines of code. In both cases, the ability to safely "re-declare" (annotate) with `var` helps make sure I can tell where my `data` is coming from, no matter where I am in the function.

Again, sadly, `let` cannot do this.

There are other nuances and scenarios when `var` turns out to offer some assistance, but I'm not going to belabor the point any further. The takeaway is that `var` can be useful in our programs alongside `let` (and the occasional `const`). Are you willing to creatively use the tools the JS language provides to tell a richer story to your readers?

Don't just throw away a useful tool like `var` because someone shamed you into thinking it wasn't cool anymore. Don't avoid `var` because you got confused once years ago. Learn these tools and use them each for what they're best at.

What's the Deal with TDZ?

The TDZ (temporal dead zone) was explained in Chapter 5. We illustrated how it occurs, but we skimmed over any explanation of *why* it was necessary to introduce in the first place. Let's look briefly at the motivations of TDZ.

Some breadcrumbs in the TDZ origin story:

- `const`s should never change
- It's all about time
- Should `let` behave more like `const` or `var`?

Where It All Started

TDZ comes from `const`, actually.

During early ES6 development work, TC39 had to decide whether `const` (and `let`) were going to hoist to the top of their blocks. They decided these declarations would hoist, similar to how `var` does. Had that not been the case, I think some of the fear was confusion with mid-scope shadowing, such as:

```
let greeting = "Hi!";

{
    // what should print here?
    console.log(greeting);

    // .. a bunch of lines of code ..

    // now shadowing the `greeting` variable
    let greeting = "Hello, friends!";

    // ..
}
```

What should we do with that `console.log(..)` statement? Would it make any sense to JS devs for it to print "Hi!"? Seems like that could be a gotcha, to have shadowing kick in only for the second half of the block, but not the first half. That's not very intuitive, JS-like behavior. So `let` and `const` have to hoist to the top of the block, visible throughout.

But if `let` and `const` hoist to the top of the block (like `var` hoists to the top of a function), why don't `let` and `const` auto-initialize (to `undefined`) the way `var` does? Here was the main concern:

```
{
    // what should print here?
    console.log(studentName);

    // later

    const studentName = "Frank";

    // ..
}
```

Let's imagine that `studentName` not only hoisted to the top of this block, but was also auto-initialized to `undefined`. For the first half of the block, `studentName` could be observed to have the `undefined` value, such as with our `console.log(..)` statement. Once the `const studentName = ..` statement is reached, now `studentName` is assigned `"Frank"`. From that point forward, `studentName` can't ever be re-assigned.

But, is it strange or surprising that a constant observably has two different values, first `undefined`, then `"Frank"`? That does seem to go against what we think a `constant` means; it should only ever be observable with one value.

So... now we have a problem. We can't auto-initialize `studentName` to `undefined` (or any other value for that matter).

But the variable has to exist throughout the whole scope. What do we do with the period of time from when it first exists (beginning of scope) and when it's assigned its value?

We call this period of time the "dead zone," as in the "temporal dead zone" (TDZ). To prevent confusion, it was determined that any sort of access of a variable while in its TDZ is illegal and must result in the TDZ error.

OK, that line of reasoning does make some sense, I must admit.

Who `let` the TDZ Out?

But that's just `const`. What about `let`?

Well, TC39 made the decision: since we need a TDZ for `const`, we might as well have a TDZ for `let` as well. *In fact, if we make let have a TDZ, then we discourage all that ugly variable hoisting people do.* So there was a consistency perspective and, perhaps, a bit of social engineering to shift developers' behavior.

My counter-argument would be: if you're favoring consistency, be consistent with `var` instead of `const`; `let` is definitely more like `var` than `const`. That's especially true since they had already chosen consistency with `var` for the whole hoisting-to-the-top-of-the-scope thing. Let `const` be its own unique deal with a TDZ, and let the answer to TDZ purely be: just avoid the TDZ by always declaring your constants at the top of the scope. I think this would have been more reasonable.

But alas, that's not how it landed. `let` has a TDZ because `const` needs a TDZ, because `let` and `const` mimic `var` in their hoisting to the top of the (block) scope. There ya go. Too circular? Read it again a few times.

Are Synchronous Callbacks Still Closures?

Chapter 7 presented two different models for tackling closure:

- Closure is a function instance remembering its outer variables even as that function is passed around and **invoked in** other scopes.
- Closure is a function instance and its scope environment being preserved in-place while any references to it are passed around and **invoked from** other scopes.

These models are not wildly divergent, but they do approach from a different perspective. And that different perspective changes what we identify as a closure.

Don't get lost following this rabbit trail through closures and callbacks:

- Calling back to what (or where)?
- Maybe "synchronous callback" isn't the best label
- *IIF* functions don't move around, why would they need closure?
- Deferring over time is key to closure

What is a Callback?

Before we revisit closure, let me spend a brief moment addressing the word "callback." It's a generally accepted norm that saying "callback" is synonymous with both *asynchronous callbacks* and *synchronous callbacks*. I don't think I agree that this is a good idea, so I want to explain why and propose we move away from that to another term.

Let's first consider an *asynchronous callback*, a function reference that will be invoked at some future *later* point. What does "callback" mean, in this case?

It means that the current code has finished or paused, suspended itself, and that when the function in question is invoked later, execution is entering back into the suspended program, resuming it. Specifically, the point of re-entry is the code that was wrapped in the function reference:

```
setTimeout(function waitForASecond(){
    // this is where JS should call back into
    // the program when the timer has elapsed
},1000);

// this is where the current program finishes
// or suspends
```

In this context, "calling back" makes a lot of sense. The JS engine is resuming our suspended program by *calling back in* at a specific location. OK, so a callback is asynchronous.

Synchronous Callback?

But what about *synchronous callbacks*? Consider:

```
function getLabels(studentIDs) {
    return studentIDs.map(
        function formatIDLabel(id){
            return `Student ID: ${
               String(id).padStart(6)
            }`;
        }
    );
}

getLabels([ 14, 73, 112, 6 ]);
// [
//    "Student ID: 000014",
//    "Student ID: 000073",
//    "Student ID: 000112",
//    "Student ID: 000006"
// ]
```

Should we refer to `formatIDLabel(..)` as a callback? Is the `map(..)` utility really *calling back* into our program by invoking the function we provided?

There's nothing to *call back into* per se, because the program hasn't paused or exited. We're passing a function (reference) from one part of the program to another part of the program, and then it's immediately invoked.

There's other established terms that might match what we're doing—passing in a function (reference) so that another part of the program can invoke it on our behalf. You might think of this as *Dependency Injection* (DI) or *Inversion of Control* (IoC).

DI can be summarized as passing in necessary part(s) of functionality to another part of the program so that it can invoke them to complete its work. That's a decent description for the `map(..)` call above, isn't it? The `map(..)` utility knows to iterate over the list's values, but it doesn't know what to *do* with those values. That's why we pass it the `formatIDLabel(..)` function. We pass in the dependency.

IoC is a pretty similar, related concept. Inversion of control means that instead of the current area of your program controlling what's happening, you hand control off to another part of the program. We wrapped the logic for computing a label string in the function `formatIDLabel(..)`, then handed invocation control to the `map(..)` utility.

Notably, Martin Fowler cites IoC as the difference between a framework and a library: with a library, you call its functions; with a framework, it calls your functions. [2]

In the context of our discussion, either DI or IoC could work as an alternative label for a *synchronous callback*.

But I have a different suggestion. Let's refer to (the functions formerly known as) *synchronous callbacks*, as *inter-invoked functions* (IIFs). Yes, exactly, I'm playing off IIFEs. These kinds of functions are *inter-invoked*, meaning: another entity invokes them, as opposed to IIFEs, which invoke themselves immediately.

What's the relationship between an *asynchronous callback* and an IIF? An *asynchronous callback* is an IIF that's invoked asynchronously instead of synchronously.

Synchronous Closure?

Now that we've re-labeled *synchronous callbacks* as IIFs, we can return to our main question: are IIFs an example of clo-

[2] *Inversion of Control*, Martin Fowler, https://martinfowler.com/bliki/InversionOfControl.html, 26 June 2005.

sure? Obviously, the IIF would have to reference variable(s) from an outer scope for it to have any chance of being a closure. The `formatIDLabel(..)` IIF from earlier does not reference any variables outside its own scope, so it's definitely not a closure.

What about an IIF that does have external references, is that closure?

```
function printLabels(labels) {
    var list = document.getElementByID("labelsList");

    labels.forEach(
        function renderLabel(label){
            var li = document.createELement("li");
            li.innerText = label;
            list.appendChild(li);
        }
    );
}
```

The inner `renderLabel(..)` IIF references `list` from the enclosing scope, so it's an IIF that *could* have closure. But here's where the definition/model we choose for closure matters:

- If `renderLabel(..)` is a **function that gets passed somewhere else**, and that function is then invoked, then yes, `renderLabel(..)` is exercising a closure, because closure is what preserved its access to its original scope chain.
- But if, as in the alternative conceptual model from Chapter 7, `renderLabel(..)` stays in place, and only a reference to it is passed to `forEach(..)`, is there any

> need for closure to preserve the scope chain of `renderLabel(..)`, while it executes synchronously right inside its own scope?

No. That's just normal lexical scope.

To understand why, consider this alternative form of `printLabels(..)`:

```
function printLabels(labels) {
    var list = document.getElementByID("labelsList");

    for (let label of labels) {
        // just a normal function call in its own
        // scope, right? That's not really closure!
        renderLabel(label);
    }

    // **************

    function renderLabel(label) {
        var li = document.createELement("li");
        li.innerText = label;
        list.appendChild(li);
    }
}
```

These two versions of `printLabels(..)` are essentially the same.

The latter one is definitely not an example of closure, at least not in any useful or observable sense. It's just lexical scope. The former version, with `forEach(..)` calling our function reference, is essentially the same thing. It's also not closure, but rather just a plain ol' lexical scope function call.

Defer to Closure

By the way, Chapter 7 briefly mentioned partial application and currying (which *do* rely on closure!). This is a interesting scenario where manual currying can be used:

```
function printLabels(labels) {
    var list = document.getElementByID("labelsList");
    var renderLabel = renderTo(list);

    // definitely closure this time!
    labels.forEach( renderLabel );

    // **************

    function renderTo(list) {
        return function createLabel(label){
            var li = document.createELement("li");
            li.innerText = label;
            list.appendChild(li);
        };
    }
}
```

The inner function `createLabel(..)`, which we assign to `renderLabel`, is closed over `list`, so closure is definitely being utilized.

Closure allows us to remember `list` for later, while we defer execution of the actual label-creation logic from the `renderTo(..)` call to the subsequent `forEach(..)` invocations of the `createLabel(..)` IIF. That may only be a brief moment here, but any amount of time could pass, as closure bridges from call to call.

Classic Module Variations

Chapter 8 explained the classic module pattern, which can look like this:

```
var StudentList = (function defineModule(Student){
    var elems = [];

    var publicAPI = {
        renderList() {
            // ..
        }
    };

    return publicAPI;

})(Student);
```

Notice that we're passing `Student` (another module instance) in as a dependency. But there's lots of useful variations on this module form you may encounter. Some hints for recognizing these variations:

- Does the module know about its own API?
- Even if we use a fancy module loader, it's just a classic module
- Some modules need to work universally

Where's My API?

First, most classic modules don't define and use a `publicAPI` the way I have shown in this code. Instead, they typically look like:

```
var StudentList = (function defineModule(Student){
    var elems = [];

    return {
        renderList() {
            // ..
        }
    };

})(Student);
```

The only difference here is directly returning the object that serves as the public API for the module, as opposed to first saving it to an inner `publicAPI` variable. This is by far how most classic modules are defined.

But I strongly prefer, and always use myself, the former `publicAPI` form. Two reasons:

- `publicAPI` is a semantic descriptor that aids readability by making it more obvious what the purpose of the object is.
- Storing an inner `publicAPI` variable that references the same external public API object returned, can be useful if you need to access or modify the API during the lifetime of the module.

  For example, you may want to call one of the publicly exposed functions, from inside the module. Or, you may want to add or remove methods depending on certain conditions, or update the value of an exposed property.

  Whatever the case may be, it just seems rather silly to me that we *wouldn't* maintain a reference to access our own API. Right?

Asynchronous Module Defintion (AMD)

Another variation on the classic module form is AMD-style modules (popular several years back), such as those supported by the RequireJS utility:

```
define([ "./Student" ],function StudentList(Student){
    var elems = [];

    return {
        renderList() {
            // ..
        }
    };
});
```

If you look closely at `StudentList(..)`, it's a classic module factory function. Inside the machinery of `define(..)` (provided by RequireJS), the `StudentList(..)` function is executed, passing to it any other module instances declared as dependencies. The return value is an object representing the public API for the module.

This is based on exactly the same principles (including how the closure works!) as we explored with classic modules.

Universal Modules (UMD)

The final variation we'll look at is UMD, which is less a specific, exact format and more a collection of very similar formats. It was designed to create better interop (without any build-tool conversion) for modules that may be loaded in browsers, by AMD-style loaders, or in Node. I personally still publish many of my utility libraries using a form of UMD.

Here's the typical structure of a UMD:

```
(function UMD(name,context,definition){
    // loaded by an AMD-style loader?
    if (
        typeof define === "function" &&
        define.amd
    ) {
        define(definition);
    }
    // in Node?
    else if (
        typeof module !== "undefined" &&
        module.exports
    ) {
        module.exports = definition(name,context);
    }
    // assume standalone browser script
    else {
        context[name] = definition(name,context);
    }
})("StudentList",this,function DEF(name,context){

    var elems = [];

    return {
        renderList() {
            // ..
        }
    };

});
```

Though it may look a bit unusual, UMD is really just an IIFE.

What's different is that the main `function` expression part (at the top) of the IIFE contains a series of `if..else if` statements to detect which of the three supported environments the module is being loaded in.

The final `()` that normally invokes an IIFE is being passed three arguments: `"StudentsList"`, `this`, and another `function` expression. If you match those arguments to their parameters, you'll see they are: `name`, `context`, and `definition`, respectively. `"StudentList"` (`name`) is the name label for the module, primarily in case it's defined as a global variable. `this` (`context`) is generally the `window` (aka, global object; see Chapter 4) for defining the module by its name.

`definition(..)` is invoked to actually retrieve the definition of the module, and you'll notice that, sure enough, that's just a classic module form!

There's no question that as of the time of this writing, ESM (ES Modules) are becoming popular and widespread rapidly. But with millions and millions of modules written over the last 20 years, all using some pre-ESM variation of classic modules, they're still very important to be able to read and understand when you come across them.

Appendix B: Practice

This appendix aims to give you some challenging and interesting exercises to test and solidify your understanding of the main topics from this book. It's a good idea to try out the exercises yourself—in an actual code editor!—instead of skipping straight to the solutions at the end. No cheating!

These exercises don't have a specific right answer that you have to get exactly. Your approach may differ some (or a lot!) from the solutions presented, and that's OK.

There's no judging you on how you write your code. My hope is that you come away from this book feeling confident that you can tackle these sorts of coding tasks built on a strong foundation of knowledge. That's the only objective, here. If you're happy with your code, I am, too!

Buckets of Marbles

Remember Figure 2 from back in Chapter 2?

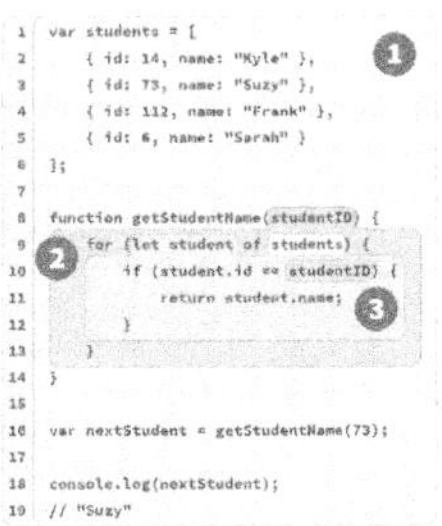

var students = [
{ id: 14, name: "Kyle" },
{ id: 73, name: "Suzy" },
{ id: 112, name: "Frank" },
{ id: 6, name: "Sarah" }
];
function getStudentName(studentID) {
for (let student of students) {
if (student.id == studentID) {
return student.name;
}
}
}
var nextStudent = getStudentName(73);
console.log(nextStudent);
// "Suzy"
1
2
3

Fig. 2 (Ch. 2): Colored Scope Bubbles

This exercise asks you to write a program—any program!—that contains nested functions and block scopes, which satisfies these constraints:

- If you color all the scopes (including the global scope!) different colors, you need at least six colors. Make sure to add a code comment labeling each scope with its color.

  BONUS: identify any implied scopes your code may have.
- Each scope has at least one identifier.
- Contains at least two function scopes and at least two block scopes.
- At least one variable from an outer scope must be shadowed by a nested scope variable (see Chapter 3).
- At least one variable reference must resolve to a variable declaration at least two levels higher in the scope chain.

Note

You *can* just write junk foo/bar/baz-type code for this exercise, but I suggest you try to come up with some sort of non-trivial real'ish code that at least does something kind of reasonable.

Try the exercise for yourself, then check out the suggested solution at the end of this appendix.

Closure (PART 1)

Let's first practice closure with some common computer-math operations: determining if a value is prime (has no divisors other than 1 and itself), and generating a list of prime factors (divisors) for a given number.

For example:

```
isPrime(11);        // true
isPrime(12);        // false

factorize(11);      // [ 11 ]
factorize(12);      // [ 3, 2, 2 ] --> 3*2*2=12
```

Here's an implementation of `isPrime(..)`, adapted from the Math.js library: [3]

```
function isPrime(v) {
    if (v <= 3) {
        return v > 1;
    }
    if (v % 2 == 0 || v % 3 == 0) {
        return false;
    }
    var vSqrt = Math.sqrt(v);
    for (let i = 5; i <= vSqrt; i += 6) {
        if (v % i == 0 || v % (i + 2) == 0) {
            return false;
        }
    }
    return true;
}
```

And here's a somewhat basic implementation of `factorize(..)` (not to be confused with `factorial(..)` from Chapter 6):

[3] *Math.js: isPrime(..)*, https://github.com/josdejong/mathjs/blob/develop/src/function/utils/isPrime.js, 3 March 2020.

```
function factorize(v) {
    if (!isPrime(v)) {
        let i = Math.floor(Math.sqrt(v));
        while (v % i != 0) {
            i--;
        }
        return [
            ...factorize(i),
            ...factorize(v / i)
        ];
    }
    return [v];
}
```

> **Note**
>
> I call this basic because it's not optimized for performance. It's binary-recursive (which isn't tail-call optimizable), and it creates a lot of intermediate array copies. It also doesn't order the discovered factors in any way. There are many, many other algorithms for this task, but I wanted to use something short and roughly understandable for our exercise.

If you were to call `isPrime(4327)` multiple times in a program, you can see that it would go through all its dozens of comparison/computation steps every time. If you consider `factorize(..)`, it's calling `isPrime(..)` many times as it computes the list of factors. And there's a good chance most of those calls are repeats. That's a lot of wasted work!

The first part of this exercise is to use closure to implement a cache to remember the results of `isPrime(..)`, so that the primality (`true` or `false`) of a given number is only ever computed once. Hint: we already showed this sort of caching in Chapter 6 with `factorial(..)`.

If you look at `factorize(..)`, it's implemented with recursion, meaning it calls itself repeatedly. That again means we may likely see a lot of wasted calls to compute prime factors for the same number. So the second part of the exercise is to use the same closure cache technique for `factorize(..)`.

Use separate closures for caching of `isPrime(..)` and `factorize(..)`, rather than putting them inside a single scope.

Try the exercise for yourself, then check out the suggested solution at the end of this appendix.

A Word About Memory

I want to share a little quick note about this closure cache technique and the impacts it has on your application's performance.

We can see that in saving the repeated calls, we improve computation speed (in some cases, by a dramatic amount). But this usage of closure is making an explicit trade-off that you should be very aware of.

The trade-off is memory. We're essentially growing our cache (in memory) unboundedly. If the functions in question were called many millions of times with mostly unique inputs, we'd be chewing up a lot of memory. This can definitely be worth the expense, but only if we think it's likely we see repetition of common inputs so that we're taking advantage of the cache.

If most every call will have a unique input, and the cache is essentially never *used* to any benefit, this is an inappropriate technique to employ.

It also might be a good idea to have a more sophisticated caching approach, such as an LRU (least recently used) cache, that limits its size; as it runs up to the limit, an LRU evicts the values that are... well, least recently used!

The downside here is that LRU is quite non-trivial in its own right. You'll want to use a highly optimized implementation of LRU, and be keenly aware of all the trade-offs at play.

Closure (PART 2)

In this exercise, we're going to again practive closure by defining a `toggle(..)` utility that gives us a value toggler.

You will pass one or more values (as arguments) into `toggle(..)`, and get back a function. That returned function will alternate/rotate between all the passed-in values in order, one at a time, as it's called repeatedly.

```
function toggle(/* .. */) {
    // ..
}

var hello = toggle("hello");
var onOff = toggle("on","off");
var speed = toggle("slow","medium","fast");

hello();        // "hello"
hello();        // "hello"

onOff();        // "on"
onOff();        // "off"
onOff();        // "on"
```

```
speed();        // "slow"
speed();        // "medium"
speed();        // "fast"
speed();        // "slow"
```

The corner case of passing in no values to `toggle(..)` is not very important; such a toggler instance could just always return `undefined`.

Try the exercise for yourself, then check out the suggested solution at the end of this appendix.

Closure (PART 3)

In this third and final exercise on closure, we're going to implement a basic calculator. The `calculator()` function will produce an instance of a calculator that maintains its own state, in the form of a function (`calc(..)`, below):

```
function calculator() {
    // ..
}

var calc = calculator();
```

Each time `calc(..)` is called, you'll pass in a single character that represents a keypress of a calculator button. To keep things more straightforward, we'll restrict our calculator to supporting entering only digits (0-9), arithmetic operations (+, -, *, /), and "=" to compute the operation. Operations are processed strictly in the order entered; there's no "( )" grouping or operator precedence.

We don't support entering decimals, but the divide operation can result in them. We don't support entering negative numbers, but the "-" operation can result in them. So, you should be able to produce any negative or decimal number by first entering an operation to compute it. You can then keep computing with that value.

The return of `calc(..)` calls should mimic what would be shown on a real calculator, like reflecting what was just pressed, or computing the total when pressing "=".

For example:

```
calc("4");     // 4
calc("+");     // +
calc("7");     // 7
calc("3");     // 3
calc("-");     // -
calc("2");     // 2
calc("=");     // 75
calc("*");     // *
calc("4");     // 4
calc("=");     // 300
calc("5");     // 5
calc("-");     // -
calc("5");     // 5
calc("=");     // 0
```

Since this usage is a bit clumsy, here's a `useCalc(..)` helper, that runs the calculator with characters one at a time from a string, and computes the display each time:

```
function useCalc(calc,keys) {
    return [...keys].reduce(
        function showDisplay(display,key){
            var ret = String( calc(key) );
            return (
                display +
                (
                  (ret != "" && key == "=") ?
                      "=" :
                      ""
                ) +
                ret
            );
        },
        ""
    );
}

useCalc(calc,"4+3=");           // 4+3=7
useCalc(calc,"+9=");            // +9=16
useCalc(calc,"*8=");            // *5=128
useCalc(calc,"7*2*3=");         // 7*2*3=42
useCalc(calc,"1/0=");           // 1/0=ERR
useCalc(calc,"+3=");            // +3=ERR
useCalc(calc,"51=");            // 51
```

The most sensible usage of this `useCalc(..)` helper is to always have "=" be the last character entered.

Some of the formatting of the totals displayed by the calculator require special handling. I'm providing this `formatTotal(..)` function, which your calculator should use whenever it's going to return a current computed total (after an `"="` is entered):

```
function formatTotal(display) {
    if (Number.isFinite(display)) {
        // constrain display to max 11 chars
        let maxDigits = 11;
        // reserve space for "e+" notation?
        if (Math.abs(display) > 99999999999) {
            maxDigits -= 6;
        }
        // reserve space for "-"?
        if (display < 0) {
            maxDigits--;
        }

        // whole number?
        if (Number.isInteger(display)) {
            display = display
                .toPrecision(maxDigits)
                .replace(/\.0+$/,"");
        }
        // decimal
        else {
            // reserve space for "."
            maxDigits--;
            // reserve space for leading "0"?
            if (
                Math.abs(display) >= 0 &&
                Math.abs(display) < 1
            ) {
                maxDigits--;
            }
            display = display
                .toPrecision(maxDigits)
                .replace(/0+$/,"");
        }
    }
    else {
```

```
        display = "ERR";
    }
    return display;
}
```

Don't worry too much about how `formatTotal(..)` works. Most of its logic is a bunch of handling to limit the calculator display to 11 characters max, even if negatives, repeating decimals, or even "e+" exponential notation is required.

Again, don't get too mired in the mud around calculator-specific behavior. Focus on the *memory* of closure.

Try the exercise for yourself, then check out the suggested solution at the end of this appendix.

Modules

This exercise is to convert the calculator from Closure (PART 3) into a module.

We're not adding any additional functionality to the calculator, only changing its interface. Instead of calling a single function `calc(..)`, we'll be calling specific methods on the public API for each "keypress" of our calculator. The outputs stay the same.

This module should be expressed as a classic module factory function called `calculator()`, instead of a singleton IIFE, so that multiple calculators can be created if desired.

The public API should include the following methods:

- `number(..)` (input: the character/number "pressed")
- `plus()`

- `minus()`
- `mult()`
- `div()`
- `eq()`

Usage would look like:

```
var calc = calculator();

calc.number("4");      // 4
calc.plus();           // +
calc.number("7");      // 7
calc.number("3");      // 3
calc.minus();          // -
calc.number("2");      // 2
calc.eq();             // 75
```

`formatTotal(..)` remains the same from that previous exercise. But the `useCalc(..)` helper needs to be adjusted to work with the module API:

```
function useCalc(calc,keys) {
    var keyMappings = {
        "+": "plus",
        "-": "minus",
        "*": "mult",
        "/": "div",
        "=": "eq"
    };

    return [...keys].reduce(
        function showDisplay(display,key){
            var fn = keyMappings[key] || "number";
            var ret = String( calc[fn](key) );
            return (
```

```
                display +
                (
                  (ret != "" && key == "=") ?
                      "=" :
                      ""
                ) +
                ret
            );
        },
        ""
    );
}

useCalc(calc,"4+3=");           // 4+3=7
useCalc(calc,"+9=");            // +9=16
useCalc(calc,"*8=");            // *5=128
useCalc(calc,"7*2*3=");         // 7*2*3=42
useCalc(calc,"1/0=");           // 1/0=ERR
useCalc(calc,"+3=");            // +3=ERR
useCalc(calc,"51=");            // 51
```

Try the exercise for yourself, then check out the suggested solution at the end of this appendix.

As you work on this exercise, also spend some time considering the pros/cons of representing the calculator as a module as opposed to the closure-function approach from the previous exercise.

BONUS: write out a few sentences explaining your thoughts.

BONUS #2: try converting your module to other module formats, including: UMD, CommonJS, and ESM (ES Modules).

Suggested Solutions

Hopefully you've tried out the exercises before you're reading this far. No cheating!

Remember, each suggested solution is just one of a bunch of different ways to approach the problems. They're not "the right answer," but they do illustrate a reasonable way to approach each exercise.

The most important benefit you can get from reading these suggested solutions is to compare them to your code and analyze why we each made similar or different choices. Don't get into too much bikeshedding; try to stay focused on the main topic rather than the small details.

Suggested: Buckets of Marbles

The *Buckets of Marbles Exercise* can be solved like this:

```
// RED(1)
const howMany = 100;

// Sieve of Eratosthenes
function findPrimes(howMany) {
    // BLUE(2)
    var sieve = Array(howMany).fill(true);
    var max = Math.sqrt(howMany);

    for (let i = 2; i < max; i++) {
        // GREEN(3)
        if (sieve[i]) {
            // ORANGE(4)
            let j = Math.pow(i,2);
```

```
            for (let k = j; k < howMany; k += i) {
                // PURPLE(5)
                sieve[k] = false;
            }
        }
    }

    return sieve
        .map(function getPrime(flag,prime){
            // PINK(6)
            if (flag) return prime;
            return flag;
        })
        .filter(function onlyPrimes(v){
            // YELLOW(7)
            return !!v;
        })
        .slice(1);
}

findPrimes(howMany);
// [
//    2, 3, 5, 7, 11, 13, 17,
//    19, 23, 29, 31, 37, 41,
//    43, 47, 53, 59, 61, 67,
//    71, 73, 79, 83, 89, 97
// ]
```

Suggested: Closure (PART 1)

The *Closure Exercise (PART 1)*, for `isPrime(..)` and `factorize(..)`, can be solved like this:

```
var isPrime = (function isPrime(v){
    var primes = {};

    return function isPrime(v) {
        if (v in primes) {
            return primes[v];
        }
        if (v <= 3) {
            return (primes[v] = v > 1);
        }
        if (v % 2 == 0 || v % 3 == 0) {
            return (primes[v] = false);
        }
        let vSqrt = Math.sqrt(v);
        for (let i = 5; i <= vSqrt; i += 6) {
            if (v % i == 0 || v % (i + 2) == 0) {
                return (primes[v] = false);
            }
        }
        return (primes[v] = true);
    };
})();

var factorize = (function factorize(v){
    var factors = {};

    return function findFactors(v) {
        if (v in factors) {
            return factors[v];
        }
        if (!isPrime(v)) {
            let i = Math.floor(Math.sqrt(v));
            while (v % i != 0) {
                i--;
            }
            return (factors[v] = [
```

```
                ...findFactors(i),
                ...findFactors(v / i)
            ]);
        }
        return (factors[v] = [v]);
    };
})();
```

The general steps I used for each utility:

1. Wrap an IIFE to define the scope for the cache variable to reside.
2. In the underlying call, first check the cache, and if a result is already known, return.
3. At each place where a `return` was happening originally, assign to the cache and just return the results of that assignment operation—this is a space savings trick mostly just for brevity in the book.

I also renamed the inner function from `factorize(..)` to `findFactors(..)`. That's not technically necessary, but it helps it make clearer which function the recursive calls invoke.

Suggested: Closure (PART 2)

The *Closure Exercise (PART 2)* `toggle(..)` can be solved like this:

```
function toggle(...vals) {
    var unset = {};
    var cur = unset;

    return function next(){
        // save previous value back at
        // the end of the list
        if (cur != unset) {
            vals.push(cur);
        }
        cur = vals.shift();
        return cur;
    };
}

var hello = toggle("hello");
var onOff = toggle("on","off");
var speed = toggle("slow","medium","fast");

hello();      // "hello"
hello();      // "hello"

onOff();      // "on"
onOff();      // "off"
onOff();      // "on"

speed();      // "slow"
speed();      // "medium"
speed();      // "fast"
speed();      // "slow"
```

Suggested: Closure (PART 3)

The *Closure Exercise (PART 3)* `calculator()` can be solved like this:

```
// from earlier:
//
// function useCalc(..) { .. }
// function formatTotal(..) { .. }

function calculator() {
    var currentTotal = 0;
    var currentVal = "";
    var currentOper = "=";

    return pressKey;

    // ********************

    function pressKey(key){
        // number key?
        if (/\d/.test(key)) {
            currentVal += key;
            return key;
        }
        // operator key?
        else if (/[+*/-]/.test(key)) {
            // multiple operations in a series?
            if (
                currentOper != "=" &&
                currentVal != ""
            ) {
                // implied '=' keypress
                pressKey("=");
            }
            else if (currentVal != "") {
                currentTotal = Number(currentVal);
            }
            currentOper = key;
            currentVal = "";
            return key;
```

```
        }
        // = key?
        else if (
            key == "=" &&
            currentOper != "="
        ) {
            currentTotal = op(
                currentTotal,
                currentOper,
                Number(currentVal)
            );
            currentOper = "=";
            currentVal = "";
            return formatTotal(currentTotal);
        }
        return "";
    };

    function op(val1,oper,val2) {
        var ops = {
            // NOTE: using arrow functions
            // only for brevity in the book
            "+": (v1,v2) => v1 + v2,
            "-": (v1,v2) => v1 - v2,
            "*": (v1,v2) => v1 * v2,
            "/": (v1,v2) => v1 / v2
        };
        return ops[oper](val1,val2);
    }
}

var calc = calculator();

useCalc(calc,"4+3=");           // 4+3=7
useCalc(calc,"+9=");            // +9=16
useCalc(calc,"*8=");            // *5=128
```

```
useCalc(calc,"7*2*3=");             // 7*2*3=42
useCalc(calc,"1/0=");               // 1/0=ERR
useCalc(calc,"+3=");                // +3=ERR
useCalc(calc,"51=");                // 51
```

Note

Remember: this exercise is about closure. Don't focus too much on the actual mechanics of a calculator, but rather on whether you are properly *remembering* the calculator state across function calls.

Suggested: Modules

The *Modules Exercise* `calculator()` can be solved like this:

```
// from earlier:
//
// function useCalc(..) { .. }
// function formatTotal(..) { .. }

function calculator() {
    var currentTotal = 0;
    var currentVal = "";
    var currentOper = "=";

    var publicAPI = {
        number,
        eq,
        plus() { return operator("+"); },
        minus() { return operator("-"); },
        mult() { return operator("*"); },
```

```
        div() { return operator("/"); }
    };

    return publicAPI;

    // ******************

    function number(key) {
        // number key?
        if (/\d/.test(key)) {
            currentVal += key;
            return key;
        }
    }

    function eq() {
        // = key?
        if (currentOper != "=") {
            currentTotal = op(
                currentTotal,
                currentOper,
                Number(currentVal)
            );
            currentOper = "=";
            currentVal = "";
            return formatTotal(currentTotal);
        }
        return "";
    }

    function operator(key) {
        // multiple operations in a series?
        if (
            currentOper != "=" &&
            currentVal != ""
        ) {
```

```
            // implied '=' keypress
            eq();
        }
        else if (currentVal != "") {
            currentTotal = Number(currentVal);
        }
        currentOper = key;
        currentVal = "";
        return key;
    }

    function op(val1,oper,val2) {
        var ops = {
            // NOTE: using arrow functions
            // only for brevity in the book
            "+": (v1,v2) => v1 + v2,
            "-": (v1,v2) => v1 - v2,
            "*": (v1,v2) => v1 * v2,
            "/": (v1,v2) => v1 / v2
        };
        return ops[oper](val1,val2);
    }
}

var calc = calculator();

useCalc(calc,"4+3=");           // 4+3=7
useCalc(calc,"+9=");            // +9=16
useCalc(calc,"*8=");            // *5=128
useCalc(calc,"7*2*3=");         // 7*2*3=42
useCalc(calc,"1/0=");           // 1/0=ERR
useCalc(calc,"+3=");            // +3=ERR
useCalc(calc,"51=");            // 51
```

That's it for this book, congratulations on your achievement! When you're ready, move on to Book 3, *Objects & Classes*.

Printed in Great Britain
by Amazon

72878461R00159